CW00344561

The Empress Codes

Krystal Aranyani

ISBN: 9798481432304

ACKNOWLEDGMENTS

Written by Krystal Aranyani. krystalaranyani.com.
Cover image by Melissa Boudreau, @childrenofthecosmos.

I bow in gratitude to the great teachers who have shared their wisdom and have led me deeper into my-self as a result. Without them this book wouldn't exist.

OTHER BOOKS FROM THE AUTHOR

Awakening the Goddess: 33 Sacred Practices
for Healing, Self-Love & Embodying the Divine Feminine
(2018)

For the Love of Self: A Transformational Journal (2019)

Glowing Goddess: A Plant Based Cookbook (2019)

Glowing Goddess: A Plant Based Nutrition Guide (2020)

The Empowered Empress Journal (2022)

This book is dedicated to all the modern day rebels daring to wildly love themselves and forge their own paths in a society that doesn't encourage them to do so.

I believe in you.
I believe in us.

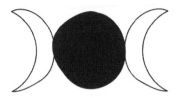

CONTENTS

A NOTE FROM KRYSTAL

Hello Gorgeous,

I want to begin this journey together by saying that I'm deeply honoured to be your guide through this sacred path of empowerment and remembrance. I don't believe in coincidences. I know you've landed here for a reason and can't wait for you to discover what that reason is!

A decade ago I was living a completely different life as a completely different woman. I literally had no voice, was in a very violent and abusive relationship that landed me in women's shelters and hospitals frequently, had extremely low self esteem, low self worth and was out of touch with my Divine Feminine Essence. I knew I was meant for something more than the life I was living, but I had no idea how to get there. I had no money, no community and no self love. If you called me an Empress back then I would've seriously thought you were nuts!

I was never told that my Sexuality, my Power, my Life, were my OWN. It took many years and a lot of twists and turns along the way to finally figure that out for myself. My journey started the day I took a one way flight to China and left my abusive partner and life in small town Northern Canada behind to begin a whole new reality for myself. Since then, I've traveled to over sixty countries alone, and after six years of full time exploring my outer and inner worlds, my path led me to tantra. After that, everything clicked. From these sacred teachings I became a Women's Empowerment Coach and Tantra Yoga Teacher (although I am always a student and learning about this profound way of life).

Tantra to me is all of life. It's a way of living that feels pleasurable and expansive. I want you to live a powerful, turned on life, Empress. The intention behind this book is to lead you deeper into your Divine Essence, to embody and love the Empowered Empress within, to Rule your Empire and to reclaim your Power, Pleasure and Passion.

These six codes were what I believe to be downloads channeled from the Divine, as the following pages came to me unplanned at a time when I deeply needed them, and I feel I'm simply the messenger to these truths that already live within you, waiting to be activated.

The Sacred Feminine Archetypes that will guide us along this journey are from the Thoth Tarot deck by Aleister Crowley. This deck appeared in my life almost magically during my most recent dark night of the soul and pulled me into the light and back into my power. As I began connecting to these cards on a subconscious level, the following codes came through. The book I use for reference is called *Mirror of the Soul* by Gerd Ziegler.

It's important to note that I share these words from the perspective of a soul manifested in a woman's body, but this book is for everyone. Everyone is beautiful and should be celebrated. Please replace any words or labels (such as *yoni, pussy, womb*) with labels that suit your reality best. When I refer to the feminine and masculine energies these are far beyond gender, they are energies within us and within all beings on the planet. You may want to replace masculine/feminine with solar/lunar or yang/yin if you prefer. As we are spiritual beings, labels aren't so important so please change whatever you'd like around into words that make you feel good and expansive (you'll learn more about this soon)!

I believe every single human on this planet deserves to feel sexy, sensual, confident and ALIVE. I hope this book serves you along your sacred journey, Royal One.

All of my love,

Krystal x

One of the most significant days of my life was when
I stopped searching for love outside of myself,
and realized I am already Love Embodied.

YOUR HIGHEST INTENTION

As I shared, I'm not someone who believes it coincidences. I believe this book has appeared in your life with Divine Purpose. I believe every sacred step you've taken since the day you were birthed into this world has led you to be here with me right now. Every step has led you deeper into your soul's unique purpose. We were meant to meet, even if only through these pages. Perhaps our souls have crossed paths before, in this life or another.

Having others hear my intentions, read my story and open to receive my message is one of the few things I take very seriously in this life. It truly means the world to me to have the opportunity to share with you in this way. Knowing why and how we show up for all the things that we do is part of being an Empowered Empress. You'll learn more about that soon.

It's with great pleasure that I share these words with you and I do so with the intention to empower you in all areas of your life; guiding you into the reclamation of your power, the remembrance of your true inner radiance, the love for your beautiful, authentic self, and the truth that you *can* have it all. I'd like this to be your official permission slip to shine as brightly as you are meant to, dare to live BIG and fully embody the woman you came here to be.

With that being said, I've stated what I wish for you to gain from this book. What do you wish to gain? How did you end up here? Where are you in your life right now that you believe the following pages will be of service to you?

Before we begin, please get crystal clear on your highest intention(s) for being here with me. How do you wish to grow from this page to the last? Write your vision and intentions in your journal. I suggest having a journal specifically for this journey into your HEF (Highest Empress Frequency). Keep it next to your bed, remind yourself of your sacred intentions often, hold your vision and declare it to already be yours.

"By banishing doubt and trusting your intuitive feelings, you clear space for the power of intention to flow through." — Wayne Dyer

HEF: HIGHEST EMPRESS FREQUENCY

They say that in order to truly change your life you must first get sick of your own bullshit. There was a point in my life where I just had enough and knew that in order to move forward I'd have to take full ownership of my actions that led to my reality. I had enough of the toxic relationships, enough of playing small out of fear others would judge me, enough of boyfriends who treated me like crap, and enough of hiding my potential to make others comfortable. I've hit "rock bottom" more than once in my life. Sometimes it takes us many times to finally release old patterns and grow from the lessons we came here to learn.

One of my favourite movies growing up was *The Wizard of Oz*, and within it there's what I believe to be one of the most important Universal Truths. After all that Dorothy went through along her journey; searching for her heart's desires, becoming lost on an unknown path, tornadoes, making random friends, running from beasts, encountering wicked witches and magical lands... she finally found her way back home.

At the end of the movie Glinda, the Good Witch, tells Dorothy, "You don't need to be helped any longer, you've always had the power to go back to Kansas." The Scarecrow asks, "Then why didn't you tell her that before?" Glinda explains, "Because she wouldn't have believed me, she had to learn for herself." Dorothy then declares, "If I ever go looking for my heart's desire again, I won't look any further than my own backyard... Because if it isn't there, I never really lost it to begin with."

Sisters, we have the power within and have all along, but that doesn't mean just by me telling you this that you'll realize it and never look back! Although fully reclaiming our power in this way sounds great, it's the obstacles along the journey that makes this life so interesting. And so, the struggles and suffering we all go through at times lead us back to our power if we continue down that unknown path with our heads up and hearts open, always searching for the lessons and blessings.

It's along that path that we discover beauty and pleasure in the most unexpected of places. This comes with a deep trust in the Universe, even when it might seem like everything's going wrong. A seed can't grow without the dark soil. A caterpillar can't become a butterfly without first breaking through its cocoon. We can't be birthed into this world without first living and growing within the darkness of the Mother's womb. The difficult and hard times are what bring us closer to our souls, to our true selves.

To me, the declaration from Dorothy reminds us that everything we're looking for is already right here. When we realize that we already have everything we desire within, we stop searching for happiness outside of ourselves and learn how to create pleasure and ecstasy right here and now, on our own. That doesn't mean that wanting more is wrong or that we shouldn't chase our dreams. It means that by being fulfilled on our own first, everything else that comes along is just a beautiful extra. We don't need it, but we sure can enjoy it!

If this book has appeared in your life I believe it means that you're currently at or coming near to the point I was when I was laying on the floor in a dark room after another toxic guy broke my heart, missing really important days of my dream career because I literally could not get myself together long enough to stand up, put on some mascara and show up. I was laying in my own guilt and shame for allowing my life to get to that point, again. I'd been through too many Divine Storms to count. I rebirthed myself and declared to the Universe that I would be better, too many times to count. I was sick of my own BS and was finally ready for some smooth sailing.

I was ready. I was ready to live as aligned as I possibly could to what I call my HEF: Highest Empress Frequency. On this dark day I decided I was going to initiate myself. I was no longer going to play victim. I was no longer going to play the damsel in distress. I was no longer going to be attracted to the guy who looked so good on paper but treated me like garbage in reality. I was no longer going to be blinded by the fantasy of how I wanted things to be rather than accept and see them for how they actually were. I was ready for better. To do better and to call in better. I was ready to align to my highest self. On this day I decided to get the date tattooed on my left wrist so that any time I doubted myself or wanted to go back to that princess mentality of lack and desperation, I had the reminder that it's simply a choice for me to rise up to the woman I came here to be. This is the choice we make every day whether consciously or unconsciously. The choice to show up for ourselves or to neglect our desires, to choose ourselves first or push away our needs, to believe in our Greatness or deny our Power.

As I sat in a little tattoo parlour in Playa Del Carmen and watched the sweaty man in a wife beater who didn't speak English draw a little crown with roman numerals on my skin, I silently told myself the intentions for getting the tattoo. I wanted to be reminded every day of the woman I always knew I could be. Whenever I had the urge to go back to the people, behaviours or environments that I knew didn't serve my greatest purpose in this existence I could look at it and remember this commitment to myself. As I set those intentions the words came through loudly and clearly; *Highest Empress Frequency.*

Highest Empress Frequency or HEF is another term for your Higher Self. I prefer to use it since Empress holds such a powerful frequency. We dive deeper into this term and its meaning in the *Empowered Empress Mystery School*, a program I created based off of these codes. At any given time we can choose to align with the timeline of our HEF. This doesn't mean at all times we'll be there or that we won't slip up. Again, we must learn the lessons our souls came here to learn and grow from.

As Ram Dass said, "We are all just walking each other home." In one way or another, we're all on our own path home, or back to ourselves, to the Divine. It won't be a straight, perfect line to get there. If everything came so easily life would get pretty boring, don't you think?

There's a point when we know enough is enough. It doesn't have to be when you're on the ground feeling like your life's ending. It doesn't have to be some dramatic, huge, life-shattering event. It can be as simple as deciding each day to choose yourself and do your best to align back to your HEF, to your soul's unique purpose or mission. To choose the people and things that make you feel alive and expansive, rather than dull and small.

If you don't have a clear vision of what the Highest Empress version of you looks like, that's okay. Read on to learn how to discover, activate and embody her.

SACRED ARCHETYPES

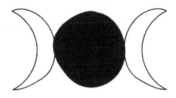

In my first book, *Awakening the Goddess*, I described some of the Goddesses in Hinduism who I've spent years working with in my personal practice. I shared how one of my dearest teachers refers to archetypes as *Icons of Consciousness*. They teach us and remind us of who we can be and how we can live.

The path I follow in this life is Non-dual Shiva Tantra. I've studied countless paths around the world and what I've learned from this sacred system is what I feel has been within me my entire life, everything I've felt to be true but couldn't put into words. My perspective is that the Divine isn't something outside of us judging our actions, but instead it's within, loving us unconditionally, because it (we) are love.

In this belief system we see all as Divine. This can be a difficult concept to grasp at first as we've been raised in environments that taught us what is "right" and what is "wrong" or "sinful". In Tantra nothing is rejected, everything is accepted. We don't make ourselves or our bodies wrong. We don't shame our desires or emotions and we celebrate the sacredness of our Temples (bodies) and our sexuality. As I learned from Osho, one of my greatest teachers in this lifetime; there is no right or wrong, only wisdom and ignorance.

When I share about the Goddesses I do so to remind you that you too are Divine. The Goddess is not something Holy or unreachable outside of yourself, she lives within you. She *is* you. My love, you are sacred. You are Holy. In this exact moment you are everything you wish to be already. You just might have forgotten this truth and that's totally okay. This book is here to remind you of your Divinity and your Royalty.

The Goddesses all live within us as different parts of ourselves we can activate at any time. Once we gain this wisdom we learn how to play with it and embody it in our lives. Just as the Goddesses are us, so are the Queens and Empresses.

Queen and Empress energy is powerful. I know these frequencies will call in those who are ready to step up, claim their throne and rule their empire. I chose to work with some of the Sacred Feminine Archetypes of the Thot Tarot because they appeared in my life at a time I felt powerless, revealing my strengths and capabilities to me. The Tarot, more specifically the Thot, appeared on my path when I'd almost lost hope completely.

These mystical archetypes reminded me of many truths that were already encoded within my being, pushed away for some time after living in an environment that encouraged my playing and feeling small. Holding a tarot deck is like holding a whole universe in your hands. I used to say that we were born into this world without a guide map until I discovered the Tarot. As I learned how to embody each of the following archetypes I share in this book, I gradually healed deep layers of my being and reclaimed my power from the situations and people I'd been giving it away to. This is why I've chosen to share them with you and it's my greatest wish that they lead you back to your remarkable, resilient, radiant, badass self as well!

So, let's begin babe...

MY MANIFESTO

A manifesto is an official declaration of your sacred intentions and motives. Write out your own manifesto stating what you stand for, who you are right here and now and what you'd like to create moving forward. Who would you like to be and what's your vision for this journey? Explain every detail. And remember to always dream big.

Define it. Declare it. Claim it as yours.

Queen of Cups

CODE I:
I OWN MY EMOTIONS AND EMBODY MY PLEASURE

THE QUEEN OF CUPS: THE SENTIMENTAL SIREN
ELEMENT: WATER

Our first archetype, the Queen of Cups, represents our emotions and feelings. Like water, she flows through life with little attachments or restrictions. She's adaptable and lives a life of ease and grace. In our society we are often taught to hide our emotions and not honour them. Maybe you've been in relationships where your feelings were treated as wrong or even "crazy". I'm here to tell you this now and I hope you believe it; how you feel is not wrong. How you feel is sacred. If someone can't learn to respect and honour your feelings, even when they might not be exactly what they want to hear, that person might not deserve to be in your life.

This is something that honestly bothers me at times, in the spiritual community some claim that it's "unspiritual" to have *bad* or *negative* emotions. Part of being human is experiencing the entire spectrum of feelings; the good, the bad, the messy, and the downright difficult. If we weren't meant to express them, I don't believe they would exist inside each of us.

Emotions are energy in motion; e-motions. They aren't meant to be suppressed but expressed. The Queen of Cups reminds us of the beauty in our emotions. She reminds us that we can use our feelings as guides to align with our highest path and purpose here. Consider them little navigation systems. When you aren't fully in alignment, you probably won't feel good.

When you feel good, you're aligned with your purpose. I know this sounds simple, but so many of us have become disconnected from our emotions and forget to honour them in the way they deserve. We feel the way we do for a reason, pay close attention to how you feel around certain people and environments.

As a single woman traveling the world I do believe that what kept me safe through it all has been honouring my intuition and feelings, even when they don't make logical sense. I learned the first few years of traveling that the times I landed in unfavourable situations were the times I ignored my instant gut reaction. There's a reason we have so many different feelings within us. They keep us safe, they tell us when we need to redirect our focus and when we need to change direction on our path. Once I began to honour my feelings before anything else, I no longer ended up in difficult or potentially dangerous situations. Amazing, right?

I believe we're currently going through a collective awakening and during this awakening we're coming back to our tribal roots in many ways. We're remembering the importance of community and having a loving tribe to offer support and guidance during our growth. When a supportive group of individuals who are interested in personal growth and expansion come together, we create a container where we can express what's going on within us openly, without judgment or shame. In a world of instagram highlight reels and unrealistic expectations imposed on us from the media and society in general, creating these sacred spaces is essential for our collective growth, empowerment and healing.

We all have emotions, fears and limiting beliefs. Every single one of us. Those who you view as the most successful, beautiful, or confident, all struggle with insecurities and challenges of their own too. When we learn how to acknowledge, honour and share what we're feeling, we naturally learn how to manage these parts of ourselves and how to move back into alignment with our highest path, or HEF. We remember that we are in this together.

When I began writing books and sharing on social media my highest intention was, and always has been, to share my personal experiences openly with others to help them along their path and remind them that they aren't alone. To remind them (you) that no matter what you're going through or how alone in your struggles you may feel at times, you're always held and supported. You are never alone in your darkness.

I feel that by keeping this intention close to my heart always and remaining open and raw in all I share, I've been met with support and have had the honour to grow a beautiful online community. I believe this is because the world is craving more raw authenticity. Humanity is desiring a deeper connection. We want to know that we aren't alone and that we aren't the only one who has no clue what's actually going on here. We want to know that others are going through the same, or similar, situations as us. The world needs you and your story; the messy, perfectly imperfect, human, you.

In her image on the Tarot, the Queen of Cups usually has one foot in the water (representing her emotions) and the other foot on land. This shows us that she honours her emotions but isn't completely controlled by them. Learning to manage our emotions and not react as soon as they present themselves is a superpower that is reachable to all of us.

We can become the non-judgemental witness of our own thoughts, feelings and life through meditation. Close your eyes, breathe deeply, and know that you're not your thoughts but the witness to your thoughts. You're not your identity but the witness watching this show of your life. You can see your physical identity as a type of avatar you're playing. In this way nothing has to be taken too seriously, as it's all just a passing adventure. This great, mysterious, wonderful game of life is meant to be enjoyed and experienced fully. How lightly and freely we step during our time on this earth is our choice.

I know that *Krystal* is just an exciting, temporary role that I'm playing in this reality and that my soul is eternal. I know that my soul is learning deep lessons through her experiences. I've come into this internal knowing through fifteen years of meditation practice, two near death experiences, and sitting with sacred plant medicines.

With the temporal nature of this world in mind, I play within it and do my best not to attach to that which can't possibly last. It's all an adventurous play and I'm the director acting as the star for a short while, so I have fun with it and view my emotions as clues into my deeper self, rather than reactions beyond my control.

In Zen Buddhism, there's what they refer to as the *small mind* and the *big mind*. When your mind identifies to something outside of itself it's the small, limited mind. The small mind is the ego and perceived self (in my case, Krystal and the thoughts she has related to her environment, as well as the roles she plays). When you're in the witness consciousness, witnessing your outer reality as a show and not identifying to it, that's the big mind. The big mind represents your Higher Self. The big mind seeks satisfaction only within itself.

Witness your thoughts and emotions floating by like clouds. Know that none are wrong, they just are. Know that you can detach from them and honour their existence rather than react or be controlled by them.

With this being said, it's important to recognize when your emotions are being held within the physical body and allow them to move through. If you feel angry go out into nature and scream or beat up your pillow! If you feel sad let yourself cry as much as you need to until you feel release. If you're happy laugh loudly, turn up the music full blast and dance wildly! Feelings are meant to be felt.

Unfortunately, the majority of us weren't taught this growing up, but were rather told to "Stop crying!" or even bribed with treats if we hid our emotions, "If you be quiet you can have a candy." Our parents didn't mean any harm, they were simply working with the tools they were given, and most likely mirroring how they were raised by their own parents. Now that we have this knowledge and know better, we can rewrite the stories for our own children and/ or generations to come.

Expressing how we feel can be fun and doesn't need to be projected onto others. When you see two dogs get into a little fight you'll notice them shake it off after as they make a loud "BLRRRRR!" This is how animals shake off the emotions that just built up within their bodies. It's natural. Get up and shake, even if it feels funny! Let any sound that comes out naturally be expressed. Use your sounds as vehicles to release the emotions held within your body. We aren't meant to be still and quiet. Shake it off and come back to your natural state as a high vibe babe! Shaking is one of the quickest ways to change your frequency.

Another exercise that really helped me when I first started exploring my feelings was to keep a little journal with me throughout the day and recording when any recognizable feelings came up. "I felt happiness when I woke up to the flowers next to my bed." "I felt jealousy when I saw a photo of my friends in Greece." "I felt anger when I remembered what my ex said to me." You get the idea. At the end of the day look over what you've recorded and reflect on the root of these feelings. Often it's not actually the perceived issue at hand, but something deeper from the past that's wanting our attention to be expressed and healed. In order to heal anything we must first bring our awareness and acceptance to it.

Stop making yourself wrong.

As we begin to pay closer attention to our daily feelings, also bring your awareness to how often you make yourself wrong. How many times per day do you push away something you want to do? And why? Sometimes we're programmed to do things that don't feel good or right for us. Silly, right? Let's make the intention together right now to claim our pleasure.

Learn how to say no when you don't feel like doing something. Make a promise to yourself to only agree to the things that are a full body FUCK YES to you, and when you have to be in a situation that might not be, can you see it as *getting* to do that thing, rather than *having* to? Can you bring joy into it? For example, instead of telling yourself, "Ugh, I have to pay the bills tomorrow." Replace it with, "Yes! I get to pay my bills tomorrow. I'm so grateful to have a home and the means to pay rent every month. How can I make paying the bills more enjoyable?" Instead of saying, "I can't make it, I have to pick the kids up from school." Say, "I'm choosing not to come because I get to pick up the kids from school. I'm so glad I have a way to drive them around and support their future."

You might be surprised how many little ways this comes up in your day and how often we deny our pleasure. The other day I caught myself doing this as I was making myself finish an audio-book that I really wasn't enjoying. Why was I punishing myself and telling myself I *had* to finish it? It was a tiny decision but deleting it half way through and choosing a new book that excited me felt quite liberating.

I'm here to tell you that living a life full of pleasure and joy is totally possible for you. I used to get up at 6:00am even though it felt terrible to me, have a coffee (which also didn't feel the best for my body) and jump on client calls. This schedule wasn't feeding my soul but I felt it's what I was "supposed" to do in order to succeed in my business. I read many books like *The 5AM Club* and convinced myself that in order to be a successful entrepreneur I had to follow the same schedule as others, even though it left me feeling drained. When I finally stopped taking calls before noon and honoured that I take longer to start my day than others, my income tripled as I had more energy and was showing up better for my clients. Learning my human design (I'm a projector) also helped a lot with energy management.

Are you choosing what feels most pleasurable for you or unconsciously doing what you've been told is the right way to do things? We all have different bodies, energy levels, emotions, beliefs, goals and desires, spend the time getting to know yourself so you can navigate all aspects of life in a way that feels best for you, rather than what others believe you should do. We reclaim our pleasure and power by making little changes throughout our days and rewriting the stories we've been programmed to believe are right and wrong.

Where are you making yourself wrong? If you don't feel like going out with friends then don't. You don't need to create an excuse, just simply tell them, "I don't feel like going out tonight and am going to honour what my body wants, which is to run a hot bath and relax with a new book." Contrary to popular belief, this is your life and no one else's. You are not obligated to do things you don't want to when it doesn't feel good for you. Self care first babes, that's how we serve the world and the ones we love best. The number one thing you learn in First Aid is to always look out for yourself first before attempting to help anyone else. That's how we have the energy to successfully align to our highest selves and unique life purpose.

Ask yourself each morning, "How can I bring more pleasure and self care into this day? How can I make this the best day ever?"

A great book I recommend that teaches us how to honour our feelings as navigation guides to our deeper desires is *Ask and It Is Given* by Esther and Jerry Hicks. As I write this I also feel called to share the first book that taught me I'm the observer of my thoughts and not my thoughts, which was *The Untethered Soul* by Michael Alan Singer. This book played an important role in the beginning of my spiritual journey.

When you look at the image of the Queen of Cups you'll notice she's barely visible with a light veil slightly covering her, this represents her connection to the subtle worlds of energy, emotion and spirit. When we're connected to Spirit, we're connected to our sacred emotions. These are our inner worlds invisible to the human eye but always present, playing a major role in manifesting our reality. The water is reflecting her almost perfectly, symbolizing how our inner world reflects our outer world. Although we may experience the same situations and environments, each one of us perceives it differently based on our life experiences. This is why we can't take anything others say about us personally, it's only a direct reflection of their internal state of being. It also reminds us that what we think we become.

When your thoughts change your whole world changes, and so do your feelings toward the world around you.

When we live a life that's true to ourselves and our internal compass, we naturally attract the people and situations most aligned with our HEF. It can be hard at times to show up in your authentic self out of fear of judgment from others, or even losing friendships by doing so. I've experienced this myself and it hurts, but to live as an Empress of your own Empire you must stand tall and proudly in who you are. Otherwise you're just living someone else's life, and you don't want that right? Authenticity is what makes us truly shine and brings the greatest fulfillment, but it may require some growing pains while shedding the layers and masks we've become accustomed to wearing. The discomfort is part of the evolution.

Empress,

Be loud. Be proud. Be emotional. Be expressive. Be yourself. Know that when you do this you will attract all that is meant for you. Trust in the process. Trust in your inner knowing.

This book wasn't actually meant to be a book, but this is what I've grown to love most about my writing journey; when the writing takes me on an unexpected ride and I naturally follow along. Originally it was meant to be a manual to read along with the Empowered Empress Mystery School online training in the format of an ebook. Once the writing began it all started Divinely flowing through, until it was a book!

One of the first images I share in the ebook manual is a selfie of me in tiny red lingerie during quarantine, when I first began writing.

Before I posted it I stopped myself, "Should I really post this selfie of myself in a dirty mirror during quarantine alone? Wearing so little?" *Yes, because I'm Krystal fucking Aranyani and I do what feels good and expansive for me.* How often do you talk yourself out of things that feel good for you, in fear of what others might think or say?

Before reading this section, pause. Take a moment and say the following out loud at least three times:

"I am _____ fucking _____ and I do what feels good and expansive for me!"

Write it out. Set a reminder. Own your damn pleasure.

What feels good for you might not feel good for others, and that's okay. As we've now established, not everyone is meant to understand your path.

When wondering if something is aligned with your highest pleasure and power, stand up and close your eyes. Say the situation, statement, or question out loud. Wait a moment and simply witness. Does it feel good, expansive, and uplifting, or does it feel contractive and low vibrational?

Our bodies are miraculous, intelligent, incredible Temples holding the Divine, our Spirit, within. They know exactly what we want and need. When our Temples feel alive and expansive, we know we're on the highest aligned path. Just as we can use our subtle feelings as navigation systems, we can also use our physical feelings as guides. This is the magic of getting out of our busy minds and listening to our internal, innate intelligence.

I repeat that what feels good for me may not feel good for you because I deeply want you to know that your path is your own. Your pleasure is your own. You must figure out exactly what turns you on and light that fire within, on your own.

If you follow my work I feel it's safe to assume you have an open mind. I'm quite expressive with my own thoughts, sexuality and I just love being naked. If social media didn't censor me I'd probably be nude in most of my posts. This is how I feel most like myself. This is how I feel most beautiful. The moment I get into peaceful nature my clothes come off, instinctually. There's been times I've done this around others before even noticing what I did. I will always feel better naked. I share some of my story with you so you know that I was born a very sexually open being. The majority of my clients (I'd say 90%) find it challenging to openly share their sexuality and sensuality. For me, it was the opposite. I had to learn how to bring my sexuality down to a healthy level that empowered me, rather than left me feeling "dirty" or overly expressive while lacking boundaries.

Because of this and my own experiences around sexuality, some that I will share in the following pages, my path will be different from yours or anyone else's. The way I feel best will be different from how you feel most authentic and confident. I want you to know that being a sexually liberated, Empowered Empress, isn't about taking your clothes off and wearing sexy lingerie in photos. For some, it may be wearing no makeup and dancing in loose flowing clothing, for others it might be wearing smokey cat eyes and dressing up to the nines in designer clothing. No expression is right or wrong, as long as we're doing it for us and not the approval of others. We are all individual manifestations of Shakti, not one of us are the same, and that's what makes us most beautiful and desirable. There's nothing sexier than someone who knows who they and isn't afraid to shine it.

Babe, own who the fuck you are. Own what feels best for YOU.

You deserve to feel good. So damn good. The first step to owning your pleasure and calling it in is creating it for yourself.

HEF STATEMENT:

Remember:

When that little voice (keyword LITTLE) creeps up and starts to question if you should really do something that feels delicious for you, repeat this out loud:

"I am (first name) fucking (last name) and I do what feels good and expansive for me!"

The voice of the Inner Empowered Empress is clear, confident and strong. She is the big you, not the little you.

I'll share more about her soon...

"I don't think existence wants you to be serious. I have not seen a serious tree. I have not seen a serious bird. I have not seen a serious sunrise. I have not seen a serious starry night. It seems they are all laughing in their own ways, dancing in their own ways. We may not understand it, but there is a subtle feeling that the whole existence is a celebration." — Osho

Life is meant to be celebrated. I say, if miracles aren't coming your way then you aren't in alignment. Simple. Imagine life as a ship and you're the caption, sailing towards your North Star (soul's unique purpose). It's never going to be perfectly smooth sailing; sometimes it'll be slow, sometimes it'll be exciting, sometimes it might even just about rock over and sink, but it's never going to be completely still. Even in our yoga practice while holding poses, we're never completely still. This existence is a great dance between energies within and around you, Shiva and Shakti.

One of my favourite analogies of this life comes from Christopher Wallis, an incredible modern teacher of Non-Dual Shiva Tantra. While I don't remember it word for word, here's the gist. Imagine before you were in this human form, you were just floating around in infinite Bliss. Not a care in the world. Everything is perfect, calm, free, beautiful. Then imagine a giant button appears, and if you press this button you'll be sent into a world of adventure, excitement, joy and connection, but in this world also exists great suffering, confusion, darkness and even death. He says it's not a matter of *if* you'll press it, but *when.*

Would life become easier and more pleasurable, if you knew that you aren't here by accident, but that you chose to be here now?

My love, open your senses and experience the potency of this moment now! Walk through life as though it's rigged in your favour. Know that even floating around in infinite bliss would eventually become boring. I know it gets hard. I'm currently writing this from a room I haven't stepped a foot out of in five weeks with zero human contact and still, it hasn't discouraged me.

At times it sucks and is even very painful. I've cried. I've eaten my feelings away. I've questioned everything. I've felt sorry for myself. But at the end of the day I know it's just a dance. I know I'm never stuck in one place or state. I come back to gratitude for this moment to simply exist and all of the gifts it contains, and I let myself get excited for what's coming. I constantly open my senses and seek out beauty in the mundane; the simple every day pleasures.

OUR SENSES AS PORTALS OF PLEASURE

This is the essence of Tantra. When you fall in love with the present moment, open the senses and learn how to find pleasure even in the mundane, your whole life becomes a sacred, sensual ritual. You don't need to sit in meditation for hours attempting to reach a higher state outside of yourself, you can reach it right here and now. Your existence is an expression of the Divine and can be a meditation itself.

We've been extremely blessed in this existence to receive infinite gifts being offered to the senses. Although they're omnipresent, we so often miss out on these simple yet profound pleasures. *Stop and smell the roses* is actually an incredibly important life lesson. It's so easy to walk by beauty and ignore miracles when we're rushing around our day to day lives.

There's beauty and blessings all around us in every given moment. Allow yourself to marvel in the mystery of this existence. Let the clouds take your breath away, invite in the melody of birds and dance wildly as the wind kisses your body, open your senses fully to this moment and experience a pleasure beyond what this physical world can offer. Reach the highest states of ecstasy right here and now, on your own.

Senses are portals to the depths of this moment, magical reminders of how precious and pleasurable this life can be. It's called the present moment because that's exactly what it is; a present. This existence, your existence, is a very rare and extraordinary gift. I'm not implying you dance through it believing it's all rainbows and butterflies. I'm daring you to fall in love with the darkness as much as the light.

When there were times I felt like I couldn't possibly go on I pushed myself to step into Nature, close my eyes and gave myself permission to feel it all. It's in those moments through our pain, suffering, or just raw openness, that we realize we have the power to return to Bliss whenever we want. It is our choice. It's not based on anyone else. An Empowered Empress takes ownership for her life situation and her internal state.

Our internal state isn't based on external circumstances. We'll never be able to control what happens outside, as I write from quarantine I really feel this. I've had to surrender deeply and trust that there's a greater purpose for everything. Mother Nature is here offering her Divine Love and eternal blessings in each and every moment. Will you choose to recognize and open to them? Will you choose to realize how immensely abundant and loved you truly are? Will you choose to partake fully in all of this life, viewing it as one grand adventure?

This is the true feminine revolution; reclaiming the pleasure we were born to experience.

RECLAIMING YOUR PUSSY

You guessed it; reclaiming your pleasure and power also means reclaiming your pussy, or *yoni*. The Sanskrit word *yoni* can be translated to vagina. I prefer to use this word or *pussy* for this sacred part of our bodies. Why? If you look up the origin of the word *vagina* you'll find that it means a *sheath*. A sheath is the cover for a knife or sword. This implies that our yonis exist to hold a sword, or if you want to imagine, a penis. It also suggests a penis is similar to a sword, when it's also a sacred instrument of love, healing, creation and connection (when used with loving intention). The truth is, our pussies and our wombs (and penises!) are the most sacred spaces on this earth. They are the space for birth and power. Whether or not you are physically able to give birth, this is a very special and magnificent part of our Temple bodies, that do exist and flourish completely on their own, sword, sheath, or not!

Now that that's out of the way, when was the last time you stared lovingly at your yoni (remember, just replace this with whatever word feels best for your experience)? I remember as a little girl spreading my legs and looking at mine with a handheld mirror. I was speechless at the beauty in front of me. It was so mysterious and brought my mind to exciting new places, wondering about the power and significance this sacred flower (as I called it back then) held.

This was before society taught me that my body was *wrong*. This was before I had a boyfriend tell me how funny it looked and how I had "cookie nipples". This was before I almost had surgery to cut my labia so it could look like the porn stars I saw. This was before I disconnected from the most sacred parts of me because I was taught to forget, and even deny, their feminine power.

We must come back to our pussies to come back to our power.

We must also, of course, come back to our pussies to reclaim our pleasure. If these terms make you uncomfortable, begin speaking them out loud. Shout to yourself, "I love my yoni!" "My pussy is sacred and miraculous!" Even if it feels silly at first. Our words become our reality, and there's absolutely nothing to be ashamed of in regard to this beautiful part of your body. Nothing. Your yoni deserves your love, admiration and adoration!

This pussy reclamation practice is simple. Spread your legs in front of a mirror and admire yourself as the Goddess you are! No matter how your yoni (or genitals) look, it's fucking perfect. I have a more prominent yoni that's very sensitive. I almost went through with the surgery to cut my flower lips smaller until a client I had while I was an exotic dancer began sending me gifts with a tag stating, "For the Goddess with the angel lips". Yes, he was referring to my pussy lips which he clearly admired. His friends even came in and told me they would be honoured to see as they heard so much of their beauty! In that moment I realized, as I had so many times in my life before, that what makes us unique is what makes us beautiful. Ever since then I've been so proud and in love with my lips and my yoni. I see it as a beautiful flower, and no flower is exactly the same. Thank you to the random admirer in an unlikely place who reminded me of the sacredness and perfection of my one of a kind Temple body.

How does that story make you feel? Does it trigger anything within you? As sisters, we are sacred mirrors to one another. Everything I share with you, you can learn from and vice versa. How you feel about another sister reveals where your own awareness can be brought to in order to grow yourself.

Stare at your eyes deeply in the mirror and honour yourself. Stare at your naked body and admire every inch of it as the most miraculous and beautiful thing your eyes have ever had the delight of witnessing. I'm not suggesting this is easy. In a society that profits off of you feeling like you're less than perfect, it will take time. Eventually, with consistent practice, I know you will get there. If you have trauma around these parts of your body then take it easy and go at your own pace. If it's too difficult, that's okay too. We are all on our own path and you know what's best for you. Again, always do what feels best my love. Your body and soul know exactly what you need.

The disconnect from our sacred yonis comes out in all types of dis-eases. As women, it's common that we have sex when we don't want to. We say *yes* when we really want to say *no*. This is often out of a feeling of obligation or duty. I used to also do this when I was younger, having "polite sex" with those who were very kind to me and I knew liked me, not because I wanted to but because I felt it was the polite thing to do. When I began working with women around the world I was surprised to learn how many others also share themselves when it's not a full body YES for them.

I don't want to deter anyone from exploring their sexuality and I'll openly admit that doing just this was a priority of mine throughout most of my 20's. I will share one thing I wish someone had told me sooner; as women we are literally welcoming our partners inside of us. Whatever energy our lover holds will be exchanged with our most sacred, deepest spaces. If our lover is on a low vibration, it will affect us. Because we are so deeply taking in our partners, it can take time to release the energies we've absorbed.

So, experiment and explore away my powerful Empresses, but if living a high vibe life is your goal, do practice discernment with who you allow into your Temple. The type of energy we absorb will be the type of energy we continue to attract, and you deserve a life aligned to your Highest Empress Frequency.

When we can't say no to sex ourselves our pussies will say no for us. This manifests in the physical as yeast infections or other bac-terial infections and diseases that don't allow you to comfortably have intercourse. I believe that intense moon time (period) cramps are also commonly our pussy and womb trying to get our attention and care. What we feel on an energetic level affects us on all levels. What we think, believe and feel manifests into our physical world. Again, our bodies are highly intelligent, they listen to what we tell them. Have the power to learn how to say no and ask for what you want. Your body will thank you.

If this entire concept is new to you and it's been a long time (if ever) that you've looked lovingly at your genitals, know that you aren't alone. Also know that every single part of your Temple body is sacred and beautiful. If I repeat myself at all in this book it's because I really want you to remember these truths.

Start by placing one hand lovingly over your yoni and the other hand over your heart. Close your eyes and breathe into both sacred spaces. Feel the connection between the two. Honour both. Know that by choosing to become comfortable and celebrate this part of your body, you're rewriting generations of stories that this totally natural part of our bodies is *wrong, sinful* or *unholy.*

"*It is my deep, hot, and holy conviction that the body of every woman is a living, breathing altar. Yes, I mean you. Overworked, underloved, insubstantially paid you. Yes, even underworked, overloved, exaltedly paid you. The question is- Do you treat yours as such?*

Think about it. There is no human alive today who was not created and held inside the living altar of a woman. We are the place where the human and the divine collaborate in creation.

Just as an altar in a sanctuary requires upkeep and maintenance to feel sacred, so does the body, woman. It is our sacred responsibility to look and feel as beautiful as possible, in order to connect to the sacred within ourselves, and shine our radiance on the world."

— Regena Thomashauer

SELF PLEASURE RITUAL

As mentioned, I'm writing this while in quarantine due to the Covid-19 pandemic and I've been alone in a room for months, the perfect time to be productive on my laptop! The aforementioned selfie was taken the other day after an hour of self pleasure and massage. I was feeling sexy and uplifted and wanted to share that energy with those who viewed it.

While I could lose my sexiness after years of being single with little sexual activity, I make a point to always keep my sexual energy and pleasure fulfilled. My pleasure cup is always full! This is a priority to me. No matter what. I've learned endless ways of how to turn myself on. Being turned on isn't a bad thing! We should all live turned on. We should feel alive and open. Not numb and distracted. Being turned on is simply feeling this moment profoundly and welcoming in the gifts it contains. Let yourself get turned on. Don't make excuses when it comes to your pleasure. You deserve better than that.

Follow these steps whether you are single or in a relationship. Carve out the time to explore and enjoy yourself, then anyone who comes into your field is only adding to an already fulfilling experience, not creating it.

An Empress is a sovereign ruler. We have the power to be sovereign in our pleasure and not look to others to give us joy and ecstasy. Dare to explore your Temple and learn new ways of making it feel delicious and empowered on your own.

Know that your naked body and sexual energy is as natural as it gets. Do something that turns you on, perhaps the following ritual, and witness how the energy feels moving through your body. Try not to label it as "sexual" or anything else you've been taught. Try to witness it as just another form of energy moving through you, just like the energy moving through your body on a daily basis. Contemplate on the connection this energy has to Nature, to

Earth, to the Cosmos. How exactly does your body feel when it's turned on? Being pleasured? Orgasming?

- Close the doors, take off your clothes, dim the lights, put on some soothing music and get ready to be intimate with your gorgeous self.

- Lay down comfortably, either on a bed or on the floor in front of a mirror. Close the eyes and connect to the breath for a few moments.

- Use your favourite yummy, natural oil or lotion.

- Begin massaging the feet. Gently massage each, sending them love. Tell them, "I love you. I appreciate you. Thank you for taking me everywhere I've been. Thank you for guiding me forward along my Divine path."

- Move up to your shins, again sending love to them, appreciating and thanking them for serving you along your path. Then up to the knees, the inner and outer thighs, take your time. Breathe into each area.

- When you reach your yoni area, gently touch the area surrounding. Rub natural, soothing oils along this area. Coconut oil works well. Do this in the mirror if you'd like. Tell this sacred area, "I love you. I appreciate you. Thank you for giving me the opportunity to connect intimately with others and to create the gift of life. I forgive myself for the times I didn't know how sacred you were. Now I do." Say whatever comes naturally for you. Stay here as long as you'd like. If you've never spent time with this area and it makes you uncomfortable just stay for a moment then move on, spending more time here the next time you do this exercise. Remember, that which we initially resist is often what we need most. This can refer to any part of the body that feels uncomfortable or even painful to touch. Listen closely to what your body is feeling and recognize what it's saying YES or NO to. Honour whatever comes up and be gentle with yourself. This is a lifelong journey to love yourself the way you deserve, it doesn't happen in one practice.

- Move up to your stomach, gently rub in clockwise motions. Thanking it for the daily processes it constantly undergoes in order to keep you healthy and alive. Slowly rub up and down the sides of your body, moaning and making any noise that naturally wants to be expressed.

- Deep, slow breathing. Moan and caress. Appreciate every touch, every inch. Move to your breasts, massaging them gently in circular motions. "I love you. I appreciate you. You are sacred." Do this for a few minutes at least. Meditate on how proud you are for all of the gifts that make you feel beautiful and give you the ability to care for and nurture others. Run your fingers up the sides of your neck and down the arms, thanking them for all they allow you to do. Massage the hands, then each finger. "I love you. I appreciate you. Thank you."

- Next, embrace yourself in a deep hug. Stay here for a few moments. "I love all of you _____. I appreciate, honour and accept all of you." Gently massage your face in light circular motions, moving from the inward eyebrows to outward, rubbing the temples, glide your fingers across your lips and moan. Open to the pleasure of your own touch. Touch yourself how you'd like your greatest lover to touch you. Keep your eyes closed, breathing in all the loving energy that has gathered around and within your being.

- Stay here as long as you desire, appreciating the perfection that you are. If emotions come up, let them. You are safe and free to express in this space. If you'd like to please yourself, do so. Let this be all about what makes you feel good and expansive. (As always;))

- Move! Allow any feelings or emotions that came up to be expressed. Dance out the emotion. Be weird. Be dramatic. Let it all be felt and then transmuted into love.

The quickest way to become powerful beyond measure, is realizing that you already are. Every single thing you are seeking is already within you. Every version of you that you desire to become is already within you.

You are what you've been searching for.

SELF REFLECTION

1. What kind of relationship do I want to have with my body?

2. What kind of relationship do I want to have with my orgasm?

3. What makes me feel most sexy and liberated?

4. How do I want to be touched, loved, and held? Am I giving myself that same attention and care?

5. How do I desire to express myself as a sexual being, within the bedroom and outside?

6. What old stories are keeping me from fully expressing and enjoying my Divine Feminine Essence?

7. Where am I holding back from expressing my emotions and feelings, fully and authentically?

8. What steps can I take now to begin to fully love and become comfortable with my sexuality? What feels good, natural, and healthy to me in regard to my pleasure and sexuality?

9. Was I told to "be quiet" or to hold my emotions in as a child, or was I given space to process and express my feelings? Explain relevant memories as a child.

10. If I held emotions in, where do I feel they've been stored within my body since? How can I begin to release them?

Queen of Swords

CODE II:
I CUT THROUGH THE VEILS OF ILLUSION WITH MY SWORD OF CLARITY & DISCERNMENT

QUEEN OF SWORDS: THE FIERCE FEMME
ELEMENT: AIR

The Queen of Swords brings forth our Inner Warrioress Kali Ma frequency. She reminds us that in order to rebirth ourselves we must cut through our fears and release the parts of ourselves that are no longer serving our highest path in this existence. The Queen of Swords in the Thoth Tarot is shown carrying a head in her hand. In many traditions (such as Hinduism where we see Kali with skulls around her neck) the head represents the ego. She has cut through the masks and roles she plays to reveal her True Self, and she is now liberated. The ego is still present, but it no longer controls her.

It's always of great importance to keep in mind that the parts of ourselves we're ready to let go of are not wrong. Every step of our journey is Divine and necessary for our personal growth and awakening. It's true that if everything always went smoothly it wouldn't be very exciting. The difficult times and the limiting roles we unconsciously play are the parts of this life that allow us to grow into the women we manifested onto this earth to be. Many of us are holding on to trauma from past lives or our ancestors. We are now rewriting our generational stories.

It is our birthright to step into our power and our responsibility to show up for ourselves and the collective feminine.

Our ancestors endured immense suffering so that we could live the way we do today. In history as we know it, we've never had more freedom and power as women to become whoever we wish to become. It's an honour and a blessing to have the space that we do to meet in sacred circles, to connect over little handheld devices and to share in the ways we are right now. It's never been more easy to connect and grow together.

Do you feel the power in that knowing? That everything you've gone and grown through has allowed you to show up as you are today? That those who walked before us paved the way so that we could collectively create a New Earth for those coming after us? Everything is happening as it should. Your presence here is already enough. Breathe that in baby.

The Queen of Swords is connected to the element of air which represents the mind. Remember, our thoughts shape our reality. Just like the sword in the Queen's hand, our thoughts can either hurt us or protect us. There's no doubt about it that the mind is powerful beyond measure. All thoughts have their own vibration. One of my favourite examples of this is the water experiments conducted by Dr. Masaru Emoto.

By speaking different words to water then freezing it, he showed how the crystals formed unique shapes and structures based on the vibration of the words spoken. "I love you" created a gorgeous snowflake like structure, while "I hate you" created a ruptured structure with a very clear low vibration. If our words have this much power over their physical environment, can you imagine how our words and thoughts affect our own bodies, which are over 60% water? As well as the reality around us? Can you imagine how our words affect the ones we love or come into contact with daily? Personally, I speak loving and encouraging words to those around me as much as I can, including my plants and my dog Priya.

Our outside reality will always agree with our inner dialogue. The subconscious mind will never argue or question our conscious mind. You can view the subconscious mind as a second, more subtle mind, or your soul, that's like a sponge. It soaks up and believes everything your conscious mind tells it.

Our world will never be different from how we perceive it to be.

"Our subconscious minds have no sense of humor, play no jokes and cannot tell the difference between reality and an imagined thought or image. What we continually think about eventually will manifest in our lives." — Robert Collier

When we tell our subconscious mind something, it looks for ways to confirm that belief in our environment. For example, if you tell yourself, "I'm not pretty enough." Your subconscious will constantly look for clues to confirm this to be true, perhaps focusing on the beauty of others on social media or TV then comparing it to your own, or focusing on the times in your life others have put your physical appearance down.

If instead you tell yourself, "I'm so beautiful and radiant! I love the way I look!" Your subconscious will also filter your environment to make this true. You may see yourself in a more confident way when you look in the mirror, you'll compare yourself to others less and focus on the compliments you've received throughout your life that confirmed you are indeed beautiful. By living on this vibration of beauty others will naturally see you as beautiful too and begin to compliment you more. This stuff works, try it for yourself! The Feminine Archetypes we're working with in this book are all master manifestors, as they know that they hold the power within to create the reality they desire and to call in all that they dream of.

You have the power to create the life of your wildest dreams and it all begins with your thoughts.

The Queen of Swords has overcome the limiting ego beliefs and now sees with penetrating clarity. She has a child over her head which represents our coming back to child-like innocence and awe for the world around us once we release unnecessary pain and/or pressure. Life can dim our light over time, but it never disappears. It's always there for us to remember and activate. Darkness is an illusion, it is simply the absence of light. It doesn't actually exist on its own. Practice viewing the world from the eyes of a child. Pretend it's the first time you've ever seen it, look to everything with awe and wonder.

When we call upon this powerful archetype or others, like Kali Ma, it means we're ready to show up and up-level our lives. We aren't messing around anymore. This transformation is never easy. It might come with a lot of pain, but a flower can't blossom then be pushed back into a bud. Once we outgrow our environment, going back to old ways just doesn't do it for us anymore. Kali is the tough and fiercely loving mother, sometimes she reveals what we don't want to see but we know is necessary for our evolution.

Call upon this energy when you're ready to cut through all that has kept you playing small. Call upon the Queen of Swords when you're ready to come back to your truest, most radiant self, letting her shine through no matter what others may think or say.

This babe has full clarity of what she wants and doesn't compromise. She has strong boundaries and makes them known. She knows when to say *yes* and when to say *no,* and states both clearly, confidently and calmly. She has cultivated strong discernment and practices it, sifting through that which deserves to be in her life while releasing anything that doesn't with compassion and Grace.

How well do you see the road in front of you? You can't create the life of your dreams if you aren't sure how it looks.

Let the Universe know exactly what it is you're calling in. When you order at a restaurant do you say, "Maybe I'll get food... but if you think I shouldn't maybe I'll change and get this... but someone else had that so maybe I want it too... I'm not actually sure, what's your opinion? Am I worthy? Should I get food or something else?" No. You most likely know what you want and order with confidence and clarity. You aren't trying to waste either of yours or the waiter's time and energy. The waiter then knows exactly what to bring you, the process goes smoothly and soon you're enjoying a delicious meal. Do the same to the Universe. Order your desires up to the cosmic waitress. Speak your dreams with detail and precision. The Universe loves clarity. Claim it to already be yours. Believe it and you shall receive it, baby. Repeat, "It's already mine." "It's already done."

With that being said, it's also important not to attach to the outcome of our dreams, fantasies or goals too much. What I mean by this is to get clear on what you want, but always leave room for the "impossible". Always leave a little space for something even better to come along, something you can't even imagine for yourself. When I'm speaking my desires I always follow it with, "This or something even better. This or something even more aligned."

Manifesting is a matter of having deep belief and trust in oneself, which entails having deep belief and trust in the Universe.

In order to call in all of the amazing things we want from this life, we must create space to welcome it in. We do this by releasing what no longer belongs in our lives. As hard as it may be to accept, some people and situations aren't meant to be in our lives forever. Perhaps they were good for our growth for a time but later began to block our blossoming. This requires you to be extremely honest with yourself and others. When we release the relationships that no longer nourish our growth, we open space in our hearts for those that do.

If there's relationships that must stay in your life but don't assist in your growth, like your parents for example, envision energetic boundaries protecting you when you're in their presence. Repeat to yourself, "Nothing can touch me but love." I envision a clear light around my aura protecting me.

View your energy like a lighthouse; you can shine brightly out to others without absorbing their energy.

Where are your current boundaries in all aspects of life? Relationships, sexually, in your work space? Stating boundaries to others is stating what works and feels best for us, and what doesn't. Being able to stick to these and communicate them clearly shows a healthy sense of self worth. It's having the courage to make choices and speak our mind based on what is most aligned (or not aligned) for us at the given time.

Oftentimes, we're scared to express what we don't want or to say *no* in fear that we'll hurt someone's feelings or push them away, when in actuality they'll be more likely to respect us for it. I know that when I've stated my boundaries to others or vice versa, it has only created a deeper trust and growth in our relationship. And if the person doesn't agree with or like the fact that you have clear boundaries? Then let's get real Empress, they probably aren't meant to be in your life. It may sound a little cold, but it's of high importance who you surround yourself with on this path. We're only as powerful as those who are most frequently around us. Choose wisely.

Know exactly what you want and don't want from your relationships and life in all areas, and hold the standard there. When you negotiate your boundaries, and therefore your self-respect, you're blocking the Universe from bringing in people and situations of a higher standard. The ones who align with your path, the ones that you deserve. The path of evolution can be lonely at times, but it will always be worth it to wait for the relationships that are in the highest alignment with your authentic self. I promise!

In the same way that we may not have boundaries, we can also develop extreme boundaries. I had no boundaries when I was younger. I didn't know what they were and was terrified to speak my desires to others. When I first discovered what boundaries meant I went from having none to creating strong walls so that no one could get close to me. I didn't clearly communicate what I needed, I just expected others to know then cut them off the moment they didn't respect my needs. This was also a result of trauma from having my boundaries crossed so many times in the past. Obviously, I realized pretty quickly that this wasn't the most respectful or compassionate way to approach personal relationships.

Healthy boundaries are balanced boundaries. This means not being overly flexible when it doesn't serve us, while also being open to others and realizing relationships take work and respectful communication. The hard conversations are usually the ones that will result in the most mutual growth and connection. Having extreme boundaries might show up as not having many close relationships, rarely letting people in, or saying *no* often as a way to feel in control. We may build up extreme boundaries as a way to protect our hearts after we've experienced betrayal or trauma. Creating healthy boundaries and close relationships can be scary, but we all deserve deep, meaningful connections that we can enjoy and grow from. Intimate relationships are our greatest teachers and can lead us into parts of ourselves we might not be able to discover otherwise.

Queen of Swords, like the element of air she is associated with, also represents communication. How are you communicating your heart's message? How are you sharing your unique voice with the world? Communication also involves listening. How are you holding space for others to express their truth? How are you making them feel comfortable to be themselves and to feel seen and heard?

We can only give others the amount of love we give ourselves. We can only meet others at the depths we've met ourselves.

There was a time in my career I wasn't showing up for others in the way I knew I could and wished to. I was allowing fear to stop me from using my voice. I had a major blockage and fear around my throat chakra. I grew up never using my voice as my older siblings always spoke for me, and I had a lisp through elementary school. Oddly enough, my own name *Krystal* is still the one thing I say where the lisp often still comes out. At the start of being online, I would cancel podcasts or big speeches when nerves took over. I have tremors and would begin shaking when I was very nervous, then it'd make me even more nervous! This played a part in these cancelations. It's actually difficult to admit because I wanted more than anything to show up for all these amazing opportunities I'd been blessed with, but I let fear take over. Looking back on it now I realize that some things take time. I put a lot of pressure on myself to do things I wasn't ready to do because I saw others succeeding in those ways.

When I realized this was a serious issue I had to overcome, I cancelled my upcoming events and really took the time to reflect on what the heck was going on inside of me. I sat with it. I meditated on it. I worked with the throat chakra and took singing and speech lessons. I asked for Divine guidance. I asked for support from my angels. I heard a soft little voice come through and tell me; *Start showing up for yourself.*

That was it. I didn't fully understand what it meant when I first received this message. I asked myself, "What does showing up for myself look like?" Furthermore, how had I not been showing up for myself? Then all these situations began running through my mind. I wasn't showing up for myself in the mornings, I slept though my alarm every day. I was only showing up to my personal practice half the time. I was skipping self care activities to work long hours, promising myself that was the "last time". I then asked myself, "If a good friend were consistently not showing up for me in the same way, would I still be friends with them?" Of course, the answer was no. I had some major self prioritizing to do.

It's no surprise that once I began truly committing to the promises I'd made to myself and showing up for myself, I then had the confidence to show up for others too. Even when I was shaking. I have always known that where my biggest fear exists is where my purpose exists too. That's where my medicine is. And my voice is my greatest fear.

Every day I do something that scares me. I believe that's part of being a human in today's world; daring to live outside of the box society has attempted to put us in so we can live the life of our wildest dreams. A life that deep down we've always known we deserve and are meant for.

Where does your medicine exist within? How are you meant to communicate your truth in this lifetime? Perhaps it isn't through your voice, but through art or movement. Creating art is important for an Empowered Empress as it's our connection to Shakti. We are meant to express ourselves and art is a beautiful way of doing so. Make your life art. Make your sex art. Make your meditation art. Make your dance art. Make your breathing art.

In her book *The Awakened Woman*, Tererai Trent shares that our voice must match our dreams. (Another book I highly recommend, by the way. She's a remarkable woman with a very inspiring story!) So sister, I ask you this, *Does the power of your voice match the power of your dreams?*

The subconscious mind is your soul, and it's always listening. Once you declare something to be true, it begins working towards making it happen. It listens to energy, not tangible evidence.

Embody the vibration you wish to be on and know two things to be true:

1) It's already yours.

2) You deserve it *all*.

The only way someone else can hurt you, anger you, intimidate you, lead you to feel nervous or small, is through your own mind. No one can *make* you feel or think something that you don't want to. You are the ruler of your mind, body and spirit. The state of each is entirely up to you and you alone. You have the power Empress, stop giving it away to others.

When you walk into a crowded room or a busy restaurant, where do your thoughts first go? When you have an interview or a first date, do you feel calm and in your power, or are you worried about what the "other" may think? (I write "other" because there truly is no *other*. *Other* is an illusion. We're all connected and of the same Source. The more deeply we come into this realization, the less likely we are to put others higher up or lower than ourselves.)

I used to walk into a room full of people and wonder if they liked me. Now I look around and wonder if I like them.

Maybe you've read that quote before, but have you really sat with it? For a moment, close your eyes and replay the last time you had a first meeting or walked into a busy social setting. What were your thoughts? What stories ran through your mind? Where did these stories come from? Are they your Truth? Do they feel innate or borrowed? How did you feel on an energetic level? How did your body react?

Quite often the stories we allow to take up space in our minds are not ours. Our thoughts are not ours. They're products of our environment, some very outdated that need to be left behind in order for us to fully move forward into the authentic, badass, unapologetic Empresses we were born to be.

"Will he like me?" "Is what I'm wearing appropriate?' "What if they don't buy my offerings?"

Whatever it may be, know that these thoughts are not yours and that it's in your power to flip the script to a more empowering story line.

Let's try again...

"Will I like him?" "This outfit looks great on me and despite what anyone else thinks, I'm going to rock it and feel amazing while I do!" "I serve from a space of alignment and know that my offerings will reach who they are meant to reach at this time."

How does that feel in your body compared to the first thoughts? I feel beautiful in the selfie I shared in the ebook version of this book. I have no makeup on and feel most in my feminine essence wearing my favourite red lingerie. It was a first instinct to use that photo. As soon as I put it onto the page the thoughts came rolling in, "Who posts a selfie in bed as their first book picture?" "What will people think?" "I need a more professional picture". Those thoughts were quickly replaced with my Inner Empress statement, "Krystal, you felt good in this photo and it shines through. You felt like a Tantric Empress. You felt like yourself and if anyone judges you that's all about them and nothing to do with you." And of course... "I am Krystal fucking Aranyani and I do what feels good and expansive to me!"

At the bottom of the welcome page of the ebook, again instinctually, I signed as "Sensual Empress", referring to myself. Again, "Does that seem self absorbed..." Nope! Inner Empress statement, "Krystal, you ARE a Sensual Empress. Claim it and by doing so give others permission to do the same. I want every woman to be able to call herself whatever she wants if it feels good for her."

Just today I saw that a guy I've been crushing on for years (we chat often but have yet to be in the same place at the same time) made a post about how he doesn't like the way women use the term Queen and Goddess recently. If you've followed my work, this is what I'm all about. My very first thought was, "Is it too late for my artist to redo the cover with a new name? Empowered Babe maybe?" That dialogue was immediately replaced with my Inner Empress, "Krystal, you resonate deeply with the terms Queen and Goddess. Not everyone will understand this and will have their own ideas around different labels and terms based on their personal life experiences. Stand in your truth and always do what feels like a FUCK YES to you. If someone doesn't align with your

Truth, they might not be meant to be in your life, and that's okay."

This inner dialogue between my Ego Self and my Inner Empress (aka the *small mind* and *big mind*) can go on all day. Just because I'm teaching these steps doesn't mean I'm beyond them. They will very likely always come up due to subconscious programming from outside sources and that's not always in our control, but what is in our control is the ability to create our Inner Empress statement, claim her words to be true, and move on confidently knowing that we are following our authentic knowing. This is more a matter of managing our ego and thoughts, rather than trying to dispose of them. The ego has its sacred purpose in our lives too.

Name your Inner Empress, or Inner Knowing. Think of a name that resonates with you and feels empowering. Call her whatever you want, she's a baddie, Goddess, Queen, Empress, Witch, Priestess, Angel, Bold Bitch, whatever! She's your inner knowing, your intuition, your authentic guide, she's your feminine super power and she's always been with you.

When you catch yourself playing small or becoming consumed by limiting thoughts, allow yourself to quiet for a moment, put your hands over your heart and womb, and listen. Eventually she'll appear; strong, steady, clear and wise. The more you practice bringing her into awareness, the more she'll appear and the more easily you'll be able to follow her guidance.

An Empress does not step away from her throne to entertain fools. She sits tall and holds the standard.

So you should not lower yourself or your standards to accept less than what you deserve.

That includes people, situations, and environments.

You decide the quality of your life, no one else.

INNER EMPRESS STATEMENT TIPS:

- Start the inner statement with your name.

- View this inner voice as strong and confident, as your intuition or inner compass, your Badass Inner Empowered Empress!

- Our intuition is instinctual. We know what's best for us, fear is what comes after and tries to talk you out of it. That first voice is usually your Inner Empress who knows what you need, the one attempting to rationalize or change your mind afterwards is usually fear from ego. Ego likes to remain small. Fear is not a negative thing, but recognize when it's not serving you and holding you back from being all that you desire to be.

- Create a name or even an art piece of your Inner Empress! Honour her and she'll reveal herself more.

REWRITE YOUR STORY

Write the limiting beliefs or stories you have, and what results from these ways of thinking. For example: "I am undeserving" = Unhealthy relationships, settling in partnerships, not chasing my dreams.

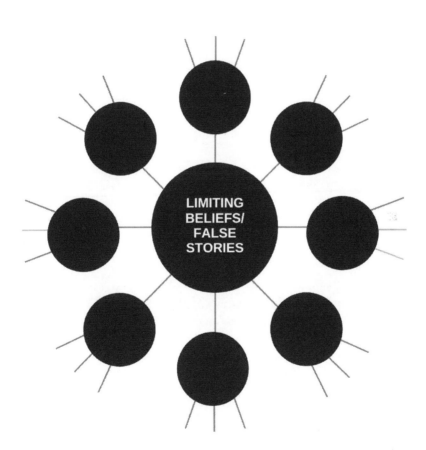

Whether you're familiar with bringing awareness to your thoughts or this is totally new to you, these tools are so important along the path to your HEF. Due to the constant stimulation and stories our subconscious receives outside of our own thoughts on a daily basis, this is a lifelong journey. I'll recommend two more books to you. I love sharing resources that have helped me because I truly want you to live your best, most joy-full life possible! The first is a classic in the spiritual world, *You Can Heal Your Life* by Louise Hayes. The second is *Change Your Thoughts Change Your Life* by Dr. Wayne Dyer. Wayne Dyer has also been one of my greatest teachers in this lifetime and I'm deeply grateful for everything he shared with us.

Pay attention to how the vibration of particular words affect your body. Try to speak words without attaching ideas to them. Just speak them out loud and witness how they affect you.

Through this practice we can learn how different words affect our internal state. Oftentimes, we're unconsciously choosing limiting or disempowering language because this is where our ego feels safe and comfortable.

Dave Asprey shares what he describes as *Weasel Words*. Words that we can remove from our vocabulary to create the life we desire. By removing these words we also affect those around us in a more uplifting manner.

Here they are:

Need: This challenges our brain (which is programmed for survival) by having it believe that we *need* many things. In reality, there isn't that much that we actually need. We can say, "I really need to go there tomorrow." But we don't really *need* to go there. We want to. We get to. We plan to. You can say, "I just *need* that dress." Or you can say, "I would love to have that dress, I'm going to work hard this week so I can buy it!" Dave says when we eliminate this word we open more space for creativity and authenticity. I think it feels much more empowering when you replace it.

Can't: My loves, if you eliminate one word from your vocabulary please let it be this! Every time you're saying you can't do some-thing, even if you don't fully believe it or you're kidding, your sub-conscious is listening and making that your reality. I find that when we use this word it's not that we actually can't but that we don't currently have the tools to, or we're simply making an un-conscious excuse because we don't want to put the work into mak-ing it happen. How many times can you replace "I can't" with "I choose not to"? Remember, you aren't wrong for using these phrases and they might always come up sometimes, but you can begin rewiring your language into more empowering stories right now. Personally I find this to be a lot of fun. Remember: You CAN do anything babe!

Bad: I removed this one from my speech a long time ago. Of course there's the odd occasion it'll come up, but I almost always quickly replace it with a more suitable word. *Good* and *bad* don't really exist as the meaning of these can be very different depend-ing on the individual. When you say something is *bad*, you might not actually mean it. Such as, "It's so bad our flight is this late!" When it's not bad that you're safe and just might have to resched-ule something that isn't actually that big of a deal. You could say, "That book was bad." When that book could help a lot of people, but might not resonate with you personally. There's always more uplifting choices than quickly putting things into the *bad* category. Remember, the subconscious is always listening and recording.

Try: *Don't try, do.* Try is another limiting word that slips into our speech without much thought. By saying that we will *try* to do something, we're instantly suggesting we won't do it. Imagine if you asked your friend to be your plus one at an important event and they said, "I'll try to make it." You probably won't be counting on them and find someone more reliable to join you. If they said, "I will make it." It's a different story. Empowered Empresses don't try, we do! And if for whatever reason it doesn't work out the way we planned, we know it's simply the Divine redirecting us into higher alignment.

I would like to add on to these two words: *no* and *don't*. I'm not saying to completely rid these out of your vocabulary as sometimes they are necessary, and in certain situations can be very powerful on their own. I'm suggesting to pay attention to how often you use these two words. I once dated a base jumper (one of the most dangerous sports in the world) and his friend who went on jumps with him told me he always makes sure they say, "Stay alive!" before a jump, rather than, "Don't die!" This is because the word *die* has been brought into the subconscious and as I've explained previously, the subconscious takes everything literally. It hears the word and does its best to manifest the command. I've also heard of children psychologists who suggest speaking to children in this way. For example, "Please chew your food with your mouth closed." Rather than, "Don't chew with your mouth open." The child's subconscious is hearing and recording, "Chew with your mouth open."

"The subconscious mind is ruled by suggestion, it accepts all suggestions - it does not argue with you - it fulfills your wishes."

— Dr. Joseph Murphy

CLEANSING YOUR VIBRATION

Practice this simple exercise for at least 5-10 minutes when you're feeling stuck on a low vibration or in limiting thought patterns.

- Stand with your feet on the ground (preferably on the earth if possible). Feel your connection to Mother Earth below. There are powerful energy points on the bottoms of the feet that allow us to absorb Earth's healing energies, which is why walking barefoot in Nature is so beneficial.

- Bring awareness to the bottoms of the feet. With each inhale envision a cleansing, healing gold (or whichever colour you'd prefer) light moving up the legs from the earth below, moving up to the hips, the upper body, to the head. Cleansing your bones, cleansing every organ, every negative feeling or thought within, and with the exhale watch it move back into the earth, releasing anything that isn't serving or healing you physically, emotionally and spiritually.

- See this light rising up through the chakras and the physical body with every inhale, and with every exhale envision a gold waterfall of healing energy pouring over your head from above, down over the third eye point, over the heart, all the way down to the earth. Inhale up, filling your aura, exhale down, cleansing and releasing.

- Continue as long as you'd like.

THINK THIS INSTEAD OF THAT!

I hope ____ happens. → _____ is happening.

I'm trying to _____. → I am _____.

I wish I could _____. → I am grateful I can _____.

I would like to have ____. → I have ____. It's already mine.

What if they don't like me? → Will I like them?

I hope they don't judge me. → Do they deserve to hear my story/ experience?

I need _____. → I affirm I have _____.

I wish this were different about my body. → I'm so grateful for my strong and beautiful body!

I'm scared they'll leave me. → I'm powerful on my own and trust the Universe brings me who and what I need for my growth.

What if it doesn't happen? → What if it does happen? How will I feel when it happens?

RELEASING CEREMONY

- Write a loving good bye letter to an old version (or many versions) of yourself that you're ready to release. Tell her all of the things she needed to hear and know in order to heal and move forward. Give her all the love she deserved. Explain why you're letting her go, and it doesn't mean you love her any less.

- On another piece of paper, write out all of the labels associated with that version of yourself, that you or others gave you. (For example, in my case it was "insecure" "slut" "party girl" "needy" "too sensitive")

- Burn those papers in a sacred fire in a safe space. Meditate on them burning as you envision all the energy associated with those versions of you burning away.

- Like the Phoenix, rise up from the ashes baby. Create and embody the new version of you. We can rebirth ourselves as many times as we like. Which new version of you are you calling forth? The Warrioress? The Creatrix? The Sacred Slut? The Empress? Write out on a new piece of paper how this new version talks, acts, carries herself, and communicates with others. What must be released in your life to make space for her? Write out all the details and begin embodying her right now. Carry this energy with you and read over what you wrote often.

ROLES WE MAY WISH TO RELEASE

The people pleaser

The *good* girl

The shy girl who can't speak up

The bitch (learn to speak powerfully without hurting others)

The spoiled princess

The damsel in distress

The worrier (replace with the Warrior!)

The slut (replace her with the SACRED slut)

The small version of you (How can you be bigger? How can you take up more space?)

Negative Nancy

The self-hater (treat and talk to yourself as you would your best friend)

The loner (sometimes this is healthy, but only if you aren't pushing others away from trauma or fear)

The excessive apologizer

KALI SONG FOR RELEASE:

Om namo Kali Kali om namo

Om namo Kali Kali om namo

Om namo Kali Kali om namo

Om namo Kali Kali om namo

Burn it all away Kali, burn it all away

If it doesn't serve us then burn it all away

(Repeat)

Oh Great Mother, we invoke you in this space

Take away our fears and fill us with your Grace

Teach us how to release our self doubts and insecurities

So we can soar high and live free

RELEASING LIMITING BELIEFS
MEDITATION

- Come into a comfortable seated or laying position and gently close the eyes.

- Let your soul know it's safe to leave your body now and go into the future.

- Witness your soul float out of your body, into the sky and come down to the house of your future self. This is the future self who has released all limiting beliefs. Who has stepped into their highest potential, stopped playing small, and fiercely chased their wildest dreams. Your future self is prosperous, joyful, fulfilled, empowered.

- Take a good look around at how the outside of your future house looks. See the neighbourhood, notice the smells, sounds and objects around you.

- Step into the house and look around. What rooms are in your house? What does the backyard look like? Allow your imagination to run wild, nothing is too big or luxurious. Only you decide your limits. Sit somewhere in your future home, perhaps by a window or outside, and take it all in. You got here because you chose to show up differently. You claimed your power and pleasure. You decided to believe in yourself even when it was hard, even when you couldn't see the outcome. You chose yourself.

- Notice who else is in the house. Are you married? Do you have family? Pets? Are there photos of your achievements or family on the walls? Notice every detail.

- Now see your future self in the house, going about their day. How do you look as your most powerful, joyful self? How do you move? What are you wearing? What's your mannerism? What are you doing throughout your day?

- Now, as you sit in your future home, close your eyes there and welcome in a new vision: the vision of your future house if you allow all the limiting stories and beliefs to play in your mind and keep you small. If you don't chase your dreams or choose to believe in yourself even when it may seem far from reach.

- Open your eyes and look around at your future house if you allow these stories to run your life. See your future self now. How do they look different? What are you doing for work? How does your future self feel and look now? How are you dressed and what's your mannerism? What does your day look like?

- Notice the house of your future self who continued to hide away your gifts and talents. What does it look like? How does the energy feel? Is anyone else there? Take it all in.

- Walk up to your future self and take a good look at them. Ask if your future self has anything to share with you, perhaps some words of wisdom from your future.

- When you're ready, walk back to the front door and say good bye. Allow your soul to soar back up into the sky and to your present body now. Bring awareness to your body and breath in this moment.

- Know that whichever future you have is determined by your choices today. Each day we can choose to show up for ourselves in little (or big) ways and that makes all the difference. Know that you have the power to create any life and outcome for yourself that you choose.

- Breathe that all in and journal anything that came up for you.

Don't just accept what life brings to you as your reality. Don't just settle for the things or people placed in front of you because it's comfortable or convenient. Dare to choose a bigger life for yourself. Decide how you want your life to look. Get extremely clear on it. Claim it as yours and then go out and make it happen babe!

SELF REFLECTION

1. Write out the stories you tell yourself that keep you playing small. What's the root of these stories? Where did they come from? After the Rewrite Your Stories exercise these should be clear. (Remember, finding the root of a belief system is important in order to reprogram your conditioning). Dig for the root (true cause or original pain, most often from younger years) rather than grabbing for the fruit (the surface problem, how it's projecting into your life now). Look deeper.

2. Write out new stories you can tell yourself.

3. Create affirmations for your subconscious from these new stories. Put reminders in your phone, write them on sticky notes and post them around your home and speak them out loud.

4. What's truly standing in the way of you living the life of your wildest dreams? Be very honest with yourself!

5. Write an acceptance letter to your ego, stating all of the things that it has taught you, and all of the times it might have stood in your way. Remember to let your ego know that it's okay to exist, but it doesn't control the direction of your life.

6. Write out some Inner Empress statements that you feel she would say to you in different situations when you might have limiting beliefs come up. Give her a voice.

7. Check in with how you're communicating with others and how you're listening. Where can you improve?

8. What are your favourite ways to communicate your unique truth? To create art? What new paths of creative expression can you explore?

I am whole

I am mighty

I am powerful

on my own.

I welcome all into my life

as a blessing

a beautiful bonus

but at the end of the day

it's me and my-self

and that is where I find

Eternal Love.

That is where I find

all that I desire,

that is where I find

Truth

Ecstacy

Pleasure

Bliss.

Queen of Disks

CODE III:
MY BODY IS A SACRED TEMPLE.
I MAGNETIZE & MANIFEST ALL OF MY
DESIRES

QUEEN OF DISKS: THE MAGNETIC CREATRIX
ELEMENT: EARTH

The Queen of Disks is one of my favourite archetypes at this point in my life. When the Thoth Tarot first appeared in my life it was during my most recent dark night of the soul. Within ten days I had my heart broken, had a kundalini awakening that left my spine vibrating for days straight and my energy extremely sensitive to anything and everything, was in a car accident on the LA freeway, got denied entry into Costa Rica where I was set to move with my fur baby Priya, then caught Covid. While extremely unwell from the virus, I unexpectedly had to drive across the USA from San Diego to Canada with everything I own, only to then be denied entry into my own country because I caught the virus. The Canadian Embassy told me to overstay my visa in the USA, which could have had severe consequences. Instead I spent six weeks alone at a hotel in Washington by the border where I didn't leave the room and waited for my test to come back negative so I could go home, where I'd then have to complete one month of quarantine.

All of these events led me to be in isolation in a room alone for months while processing trauma on all levels. I laid in bed and worked with this Tarot deck for hours upon hours every day. I took courses and meditated on the images. It was a healthy distraction, and at the same time pulled me deeper into my-self as I discovered new ways to heal. This book was also a result of that fruitful darkness. I share these experiences to let you know that things aren't always going to go perfectly smoothly, unexpected and challenging events happen, but there's always new, creative ways out of the darkness if you remain open to them. I share my experiences because I know so many of us have been affected by the pandemic and have had our lives uprooted and rerouted in unexpected ways.

This archetype consistently appeared every day through that process. The Queen of Disks is sitting on her juicy, giant pineapple looking back on the winding road along the arid desert that led her to this point now. This felt like my reality when I finally reached Canada and found a beautiful space to grow and witness my dreams come into fruition, all while looking back on the desert and winding road that was my time in California. I literally looked back at the desert through my rear view window on that drive and knew big, beautiful things were waiting for me once I reached my destination and all of those obstacles were in the past. That drive challenged me on all levels, especially my physical body. I would explain more, but it was graphic. My poor little sensitive Priya had to witness me through it all, and also love me so unconditionally.

My steering wheel felt a lot of tears on that trip. Driving became the hardest thing I ever had to do and took every ounce of energy I had. At one point I pulled over on the long straight highway and got sick for about the twelfth time that day. I was near a tall yellow grass field and collapsed to my knees. I let my forehead fall to the earth and began sobbing. I lost all hope. I felt so alone. My heart was broken, my physical body was shutting down, and my mental health was deteriorating every mile I drove in that state of pain and utter exhaustion.

When I lifted my head back up my eyes focused on a big black cat with bright yellow eyes sitting in the bush about ten feet directly in front of me. It felt like we were miles from any residential area so its presence surprised me. Our eyes met immediately and I couldn't look away. It's like I was hypnotized, she just stared into my soul and didn't move. We kept eye contact for at least four minutes as she remained still and expressionless and I ugly cried to her. Seriously, I was wailing. It was a profound moment for me. I felt a mystical, powerful Divine Feminine energy from this mysterious black cat. I'd never had an animal keep my gaze so long and steadily. I felt seen and supported as I let everything I'd been holding in for the past thousand miles release while we witnessed one another, in our very different flesh suits but similar wild spirits.

I got back in my SUV that was filled to the brink with my belongings, closed my eyes and meditated on what happened. I felt she
was a message from the Universe to believe in the mystical and
remember the magical. Even in our most difficult moments, there
is magic to be found. There is power to be discovered. There is
beauty all around. We are always being held by the Universe, the
elements, the Earth and the cosmos. We so often feel alone while
forgetting to slow down and truly open to the beings and life
around us offering their presence and support. I believe it was that
cat and her precious reminder that got me through the rest of the
trip. I had hope again that there was a brighter tomorrow just
around the corner.

This is one of the keys for getting through the tough times, remembering that they're only temporary and trusting that better
days are ahead. We're never stuck in one place or state, but sometimes we may convince ourselves otherwise.

The Queen of Disks is the only Queen looking backwards. It's okay
to look back on our past but I make a point of only doing so to remember and celebrate how far I've come. What's back there has no
place in our future. It's behind us for a reason. It got us to where
we are today and that makes it all Divine, but there's no need to
dwell on it or allow it to affect our vibration now. Remember,
some people and things aren't meant to come along for the new
chapters of our lives. Look back with acceptance and grace, and
claim your throne in the present.

The pineapple represents our desires and dreams coming into
fruition. The horns on the Queen's head represent enlightenment,
clarity and a higher perspective. The goat in front of her is associated with Capricorn; tenacious, independent and determined. This
Queen isn't afraid to put in the time and work to get to where she's
going, a trait of Capricorn. She knows that in order to harvest
one's deepest desires it often takes great determination and focus.
She's willing to keep showing up even when it's difficult and
messy. She doesn't believe that manifesting is only sitting around
wishing for something, but knows that it also requires inspired,
consistent action.

Even though her road wasn't always perfectly straight, she knew where she was going and didn't give up on herself or her dreams, no matter who or what might've attempted to get in her way. This Queen represents everything in our physical world including our bodies, material belongings and Earth. She is Shakti. Everything that makes up our tangible reality can be viewed as different forms of Shakti manifested into physical form, therefore none of this physical world is *wrong* (or *bad* as we just learned). In Tantra we learn that everything is Divine in its own special way. She reminds us to take the highest care of our Temples, nourishing them with high vibrational foods from the earth, exercising and doing all of the things that feel expansive and good for our miraculous bodies that do so much for us!

There's a lot of blockages and limiting beliefs around money in the spiritual community. It's often viewed as wrong or "the root of all evil". The truth is, money is innocent. It's a tool, and how it's used is up to the person using it. I deeply believe that we're meant to be abundant on all levels and there's enough to go around for all. Prosperity is our birthright. Again, there's nothing wrong with materials. There's nothing wrong with desiring a luxurious lifestyle and beautiful things. There's nothing wrong with wearing makeup and caring about how you look. There's nothing wrong with this physical world.

So often we hear of money or outer beauty as being unspiritual. Caring about our outer beauty and enhancing it in a way that makes us feel more attractive has always existed in society. Also, in order to do a lot in this world or make the greatest impact, you most likely do need to have money. If you're reading this book it's likely that you care about the world and being a better person. It's people like you who need to have the money to do that, not those who are using it for personal greed and control.

When I first committed to a spiritual path I began staying in ashrams and exploring spiritual communities around the world. I completely stopped wearing makeup and sold all of my clothes so I owned nothing except two medium sized suitcases (and my painting of Kat, you'll learn about her soon). I believed what many do on a religious or spiritual path; that we can't have material abundance and be spiritual at the same time. I believed that I needed to choose between living an abundant lifestyle and caring for my physical appearance, or living the life of a yogi in the ashram. I felt I needed to renounce all worldly life in order to be a good person.

This belief of course comes from the idea that anything outside of ourselves is not real; that the eternal soul within is the Divine and our True Self. So then why are we here, living in this world where you do require money to make an impact or just live life smoothly? Why would our identities and egos exist if they were wrong? I watched my parents stress about bills the first week of every month and declared at a young age that would never be me.

As I followed a more yogic lifestyle, I felt lost and perplexed. Not wearing makeup or clothes that made me feel sexy and feminine made me feel like someone other than myself. It didn't feel empowering to be making only enough money to get by or not knowing how to take control of my financial situation. I felt small in bank meetings and disempowered when I checked my bank balance. There were times I sat in the grocery store parking lot crying that my card was declined again and I wouldn't be able to eat that day. That didn't feel very "spiritual" to me, to say the least.

Having worked as a model and exotic dancer, I still had friends in both industries who loved dressing up and going out. When I'd visit them I wouldn't have anything to wear and felt out of place. People at upscale events would look at me like I'm an alien with my loose hippy clothing and long dreadlocks. When I'd go back to the ashrams and even wore a little bit of mascara I'd be judged for wearing makeup and be asked why I was dressing up to meditate. As much as I loved my friends in both worlds, something didn't feel right and I felt like I was being untrue to myself. I took others' judgments personally because I didn't know who I was yet.

Eventually my path led to tantra and I'm deeply grateful for it. As I've already shared, Tantra doesn't reject anything. It accepts everything. We can be part of the world, just not of it. What this means is that we can play in this material world but not mistake it for our identity or take it too seriously. We deserve to live abundantly, but if the number in your bank account suddenly changes tomorrow it won't affect who you are as a person. We are all spiritual beings. No one is more spiritual than another, but we can be more connected and aware of our spirit than others.

To me, *spiritual* means *spirit-ritual*. To be spiritual is to come back to Spirit a little each day in sacred, aware, ritual. You can absolutely do that whether you're a monk or a billionaire. And not to put down monks in any way as every monk I've ever met has been a compassionate, caring being, but when I first stayed with Buddhist monks I began to feel selfish in our daily practices. What's more of service to this world, becoming a millionaire and helping to uplift others with that money, or sitting in Nature meditating alone every day? Of course we can't ever compare two individual life purposes, and both scenarios do uplift the collective as we're all connected, but I'm sharing this to show you that you can be spiritual and of service to the world while being in the world.

At the start of the pandemic I had retreat centres I was meant to hold events in keep the money I invested in our upcoming events and go MIA on me. Their websites were gone and phone numbers disconnected. I had many clients take back their nonrefundable deposits after the third-party allowed them to, against my terms and conditions that they had previously agreed to and signed for. My business and life took a massive hit, as it did for many others in 2020. Other obstacles were presented at the same time that shocked my nervous system and brought my bank from the highest savings I've ever had, to negative. Overnight.

Times became pretty tough my loves. I was living in survival mode and had to be very conscious of not allowing myself to fall into victimhood. I was hurt by the sisters who knew how the situation would affect me but still chose to take the money back. I was hurt by myself for not setting up a better system to protect me if something like this were to happen. Although it was a dark time, I didn't let it affect who I am or how I show up in the world. It allowed me to brainstorm and discover new ways to call in money. And most importantly, it humbled me. I learned how to ask for help and support. I realized I'd been caught up in the numbers not only in my bank but also on social media. How many likes I was getting and how high my engagement was. I was identifying with things outsides of myself that were out of my control. I knew better than that. This past year was a huge reminder to commit to coming back to my true self (Spirit) each day and know that is what's real. Again, everything else is just a beautiful bonus!

Having money allows us to help others more. When you're creating your abundance vision and dreams, remember to add in some goals regarding the collective. Perhaps helping your neighbour with the bills one month or donating to your favourite charity. I believe we're here to serve and no matter how much money you have, if you have it alone you aren't going to truly enjoy it. The more we give the more we can receive. Learning how to manage our money and obtain financial freedom, which also looks different for everyone, is another form of independence and empowerment. I believe our whole world would transform if the feminine became financially empowered.

As much as we push it away, we are living in a material society. Unless you grew up out in the bush away from civilization, you've been influenced by your environment. I don't want us to shame this part of our lives anymore. I want us to embrace it! Again, intention is everything. Sometimes on social media I'll post a photo looking done up or wearing designer panties, lingerie is the one thing I splurge on as it feels fabulous having great quality, sexy undergarments. The comments will roll in, "I thought you were supposed to be spiritual?" "Wow great spiritual guru wearing designer." "Are you a yoga teacher or lingerie model?" I'll admit it usually sounds a bit nastier than that, but you get the idea.

I've never called myself a guru or spiritual teacher. This is what some people have decided to view me as, then become upset when I don't fit into the idea they've created of me in their own minds. I'm just me. Sharing my story with the intent to help others. You're just you. People will always judge us if they haven't accepted parts of themselves. That has nothing to do with us. The sooner you accept this the sooner you'll find peace within yourself, as well as give yourself full permission to be yourself! Which feels pretty damn amazing.

I used to allow these comments to get to me, I'll admit. I used to only post photos that I felt were aligned with how others viewed me so I could avoid judgment. I didn't want to appear materialistic. I didn't want to share my financial success or wear designer clothing, because I wouldn't look spiritual. Eventually I stopped giving a shit. Caring what others think about you is so exhausting! Why was I making their opinions so much more important than doing what feels best for me anyway? I started expressing myself fully and it feels so much better.

I'm a 31 year old woman who felt inadequate for the first 23 years of her life because she was raised in a society that profits off of low self esteem and disconnection from Spirit. I worked as a model and was obsessed with the fashion industry at a very young age. For the first 18 years of my life I wanted to be a famous model. I was raised with heavy media influence and constantly compared myself to the women on TV and on the front of magazines. I believed the messages I received from the media, which told me that I had to look a certain way and have a certain amount of things, and continue acquiring more things constantly, in order to be happy.

I broke out of that society for many years and lived in East Asia. I follow a spiritual path and am committed to my daily practice. I've come a long way when it comes to releasing my ego and self doubts, but if I continue to push away the parts of me that heavily existed for those first 23 years of life on this earth, and pretend I'm unaffected by the vibrations I'm exposed to every day, I'm suffering. I'm pushing away parts of who I am and the things I identified with for many years. I'd rather be perfectly imperfect. I'd rather love myself where I am right now and do my best to be a little better each day.

Maybe there's some conditioning I can't release fully in this lifetime, but because I'm aware of this I can teach my future children or those I come into contact with, that there's a different way. That they don't need to be or look a certain way to be happy. That being themselves is the best and most beautiful thing they could ever be. I can teach them what I wasn't taught as a young girl and they can shift the future for our bloodlines and teach others around them. We are all products of our society on some level, whether we like it or not. Wouldn't life be a lot easier if we celebrated that rather than viewed it as wrong? Or spend our energy trying to pretend that we're something we aren't?

Spiritual bypassing is a common way of hiding the parts of us that we are ashamed of, or are not yet ready to embody. If you ever go to a spiritual event in LA you'll most likely meet all types of spiritual bypassing and suppressed anger or sadness. (Sorry if I'm calling anyone out, but I always promise to be real with you!) People discover spirituality and use it as armour to hide what's really going on inside, even labeling and identifying themselves as a spiritual teacher. This is actually the opposite of spirituality; covering it up with an identity. It's more spiritual to be a lawyer in a $4000 suit fully aware of her-self and embodying it, approaching her work from a space of service, than to watch The Secret, wear a mala necklace, and become a self proclaimed spiritual teacher who only preaches love and light while bypassing their true inner emotions.

I believe this type of message to be detrimental to the generations coming. Believing we must be happy and positive all the time is not spiritual or healthy. I make a point of this because I know that if sixteen year old Krystal saw good looking spiritual teachers in California preaching love and light, saying they never have bad days, and sharing their new sports car they apparently just manifested out of thin air, I would've honestly hated my life to the point of wanting to end it. I know that sounds dramatic, but I was a sensitive little sponge back then and already had so much to deal with at school and home. I feel blessed that social media wasn't yet a thing while I was in high school. My introduction to spirituality was through discovering Gandhi and spending my afternoons after school studying about him in the local library.

"Positive thinking is simply the philosophy of hypocrisy – to give it the right name. When you are feeling like crying, it teaches you to sing. You can manage if you try, but those repressed tears will come out at some point, in some situation. There is a limitation to repression. And the song that you were singing was absolutely

meaningless; you were not feeling it, it was not born out of your heart." – Osho

My hope for all of us as feminine leaders is to be as authentic and empowering as we can, with the younger generations in mind. I'm not suggesting I'm above any of the aforementioned characteristics. In ways I'm calling my own self out too. I try my best to be aware of my actions and to be honest with myself when I'm acting from the ego and from the heart space.

Be very honest with yourself about who you are, where you currently are in life and do your best to love yourself right here and now. Do your best to allow that beautiful being to shine through from the heart. When we are fully ourselves we give others permission to be fully themselves too.

The Queen of Disks week in Empowered Empress Mystery School is our magnetic manifesting week. When we begin to embrace and embody our true selves fully, and align to our HEF, we become magnetic to all that we desire. It does require action, however. While the Law of Attraction does of course work, I'm someone who believes in intentional action and working for our dreams as well. This is the balance of the feminine (receptive) and masculine (action).

Never underestimate your ability to dream up worlds and therefore create them. Nothing is holding you back from a life of your wildest dreams, except most likely yourself and your own thoughts. Read that again. When you infuse imagination with powerful intention and act from there, worlds are created. Get excited for what's coming babe. Act like it's set in stone. Your dreams are inevitable.

When I took that hit at the start of the pandemic I switched my self pity (Libra's shadow self) for excitement. I'd say, "I'm so excited I'm about to be a millionaire! I'm so excited for my success just around the corner! I'm ecstatic about my big launch soon! I'm so grateful for my new success!" I allowed myself to truly get so excited until I felt like my heart was leaping out of my chest. I also took all kinds of different money courses to establish a healthier relationship with my finances. We can't manifest that which we believe to be wrong! Always remember my love: being grateful will attract more to be grateful for.

The whole world is abundant and full of unlimited resources, so how can so many of us live in a scarcity and lack mindset? Of course, this mentality is usually passed down through generations when they did live in extreme scarcity. You can never learn everything there is to learn, you can never have everything there is to have, and you can never have all of the money in the world, the possibilities of what your life can be are endless. We literally live in a world of unlimited potential and abundance, so start believing it and tap into it. Get out there and claim your riches, Empress!

"We must be convinced that abundance is the natural state of the Universe. To experience and accept abundance in our life, we must be convinced that as we conceive and believe, the Universe handles the details." — Ernest Holmes

LET'S TALK MONEY, HONEY.

Reflect on the following questions: What's your current relationship with money? If money were your partner, would it feel loved, neglected, disrespected, appreciated...? What beliefs do you carry around money and outward success from your parents or childhood environment? Your bank statement is a reflection of your beliefs around money and your own self worth. Where is it now? Where would you like it to be? How confident do you feel managing your finances? How are you planning for your financial future?

After years of financial training, business courses and creating my own multi-six figure businesses through A LOT of trial and error, my path more recently has led me to empowering women in the areas of money and business. I received a clear message from Source that by empowering women to create and run their own Empires I would be giving them the tools to change the world. My ultimate goal in this existence is to raise the vibration of the collective and create the biggest wave of love possible.

Our societies and those in power have been overly masculine for a long time in our history. There's nothing wrong with the masculine when it's at a healthy level, but currently it's toxic. This feminine rising era isn't about the feminine energy overpowering the masculine, but rising back to meet it in balance. (Reminder that these energies do not automatically mean female and male. These are energies beyond the physical. It's a little confusing I know, but this is just how we choose to label them.)

When women come into their power financially, they have more opportunity to heal the world.

At the end of the day, money is energy. As I mentioned, it's innocent on its own. It's what those who have it choose to do with it that determines how this energy affects the world or others around it. View money like a baseball bat. A bat can be used to come together with community and play a sport you love, or it could be used to break something or even hurt someone. Either way, the bat itself is innocent. It's just a tool. If you are a loving human who cares about the world then you are one of the humans on this planet who could benefit it by having more money. As with everything in this physical world, just like sex and power, intention is everything.

An example of common limiting money beliefs are:

Money doesn't grow on trees. You have to work really hard to make money. You aren't worthy of money so spend it as you make it. I'm unworthy of money and success. I'm not good with money. Money doesn't buy happiness. Money is the root of all evil. People with money are bad or stuck up. More money means more problems or more taxes. Others will judge me or look at me differently if I have a lot of money. I can't manage large amounts of money responsibly. You have to hold onto money when you have it. Money is unspiritual. Having more than I need is greedy. If I make more money others will have less. People in my life will feel bad if I make more money than they do.

Did any of those resonate with you? If so, it's okay! It's normal babe. There's been a lot of confusion and deep rooted beliefs around money. Luckily, we're blessed to live in the information age where all we have to do is Google "How to invest" "How to understand credit cards" "How to manage my bank accounts" and unlimited resources will appear! If you don't currently have the funds to invest in money management and mindset coaching or courses, I recommend hopping on YouTube and researching these topics. It's a very powerful feeling to know how to manage your money and release confusion around where it's going and how it's benefiting you. Make money your lover!

How well do you receive? As I mentioned, the feminine is receptive. Imagine the egg before the sperm reaches her, she's sitting there on her little throne while the millions of sperm cells fight to reach her. When we make love we receive our partners. It's Nature. How well do you receive compliments? Do you allow others to offer you gifts and services easily? Do you allow others to open doors for you or go out of their way to make your life easier? Begin paying attention to how well you receive. The next time someone opens the door or compliments you, pause for a moment, take it all in, then thank them. Whenever money, no matter the amount, is deposited into your bank account, open your arms wide and say, "Thank you, thank you, thank you! I open to receive and am grateful for it all!"

My dog (and best friend!) Priya has taught me a lot about how manifesting works.

When she first came into my life I brought her for morning walks the first few days in a row followed by a treat. The following days I didn't mention a treat to her, but she'd come home jumping around and wagging her tail so expectantly that I couldn't ignore her and say no. Now, years later, Priya still gets her treat every morning after we go for our walk. When you're celebrating already, life wants to give you that which you desire. It comes easily.

Remember that when we refer to the Universe, we're also referring to ourselves and others, since we are the Universe embodied in this physical reality. Therefore, when we're joyful and excited, we do what we can to stay on that vibration because it feels good. When we're celebrating what's on its way to us and wholeheartedly trust that it's coming, we make it happen, or the Universe gives it to us! It's easy to give to someone who is already on the vibration of receiving.

Priya also trusts me to take care of her and provide for her so it's easy to do so. If she were running around, not listening when I ask her to do things so I can best serve her, it would be really hard to take care of her. It would also be difficult to know what she needs if she was all over the place and not sure what to ask for. When she's hungry, she goes by her dish. When she wants to go outside, she goes by the door. When she wants pets, she rolls over on her back and expects me to pet her belly. She has no blocks when it comes to receiving!

Maybe you're understanding this comparison or maybe you're thinking it's silly, but either way it's a reminder that in order to manifest our desires, we must expect that they're coming, celebrate them before they arrive, be very clear with what it is we desire, and ask for it. Thanks for these sacred lessons, Priya!

Books I recommend on wealth consciousness:

The Abundance Book, John Randolph Price

Secrets of the Millionaire Mind, T. Harv Eker

Rich Dad Poor Dad, Robert Kiyosaki

The Science of Getting Rich, Wallace D. Wattles

You're a Badass at Making Money, Jen Sincero

Think and Grow Rich, Napoleon Hill

Money Master the Game, Tony Robbins

ABUNDANCE AFFIRMATIONS

I am the Source of my own Abundance.
I am Abundance embodied. I AM Abundance.
Prosperity is my birthright.
I love money and money loves me.
My net worth doesn't determine my worth.
Abundance comes from within.
I am a wealthy woman.
I am worthy of prosperity and success.
Money flows to me easily from all directions.
I deserve all of my wildest desires and then some.
Money flows to me quickly and easily.
Money is always coming to me in new ways.
I am a money magnet!
Divine riches pour into my life.
I release the mentality of lack,
I return to my Divinity.
I always have more than enough.
I am aligned with the frequency of Abundance.
I use money to better my life and others' lives.
I use money to make the world a better place.
Abundance is my natural state.
I trust myself with money. I trust myself with massive success.
It is safe to be all that I came to this earth to be.
I am wide open to receiving:
More money!
More love!
More opportunities!
More pleasure!
More grace!
More fun!
More play!
More abundance!
More fulfillment!

PRACTICES TO STRENGTHEN YOUR RELATIONSHIP WITH MONEY

- Practice Abundance affirmations daily.

- Bring your awareness to your internal dialogue around money and switch it to more positive stories.

- Check your bank account daily, don't shy away from the statements. Always know the state of your finances.

- Show appreciation for every single payment you receive. Your subconscious doesn't know the difference between a penny and one million dollars.

- Respect all money. Even pennies, dimes, etc. Celebrate riches in every form! Collect and appreciate all the money you find.

- Change your attitude from *having to* pay for things to *getting to*, such as; "I have to pay the bills" to "I get to pay the bills! I'm so grateful to have shelter and food." Whenever you have a bill, list all of the things you're grateful for that it gives to you. (Electricity to see, eat and live, water to bathe, shelter, etc!) Not everyone has the luxury of paying monthly bills to access this standard of living.

- Get crystal clear on your financial goals.

- Explore new ways to make money and invest.

- Attend our Empowered Empress training or a money training with another teacher you feel called to! Always have a beginner's mind and be willing to learn from others' experiences.

- Spend time around people who are wealthy and have a healthy relationship with money.

- Read books and listen to podcasts about money and abundance.

- Treat your purse and wallet like an altar; clean, organized and sacred.

- Write a love letter to money. Make sure your money knows how much it's appreciated!

- Treat yourself. Invest in yourself. Don't cheap out on the things you truly desire that will uplift you in healthy ways. Embody wealth. Money attracts money.

- Put a bill on your altar and view money as a sacred energy.

- Claim it! Write all over the place the exact amount you are calling in.

- Know that your value is not determined by a number and that you ARE abundance embodied.

- Practice forgiving yourself for past spending or acquiring debt.

- Practice the 3-6-9 method every morning: Write down your desire 3 times. Write down your why 6 times. Repeat your desire 9 times.

- Create a money celebration playlist, dance to it, open your arms wide and energetically receive all the wealth and abundance that you already have and that's on its way! (My favourite song for this is *Money* by Pink Floyd, I listen to it often and visualize money in my hands and all around me!)

LIVE YOUR DREAMS NOW

While manifesting your biggest, wildest dreams, use the following script. I learned this in my NLP training and I follow it for all of my goals. The more specific the better.

It is now _____

And I have/am _____

I know this because I see _____

I hear _____

I feel _____

And I achieved this because I _____

Example:

It is now October 18, 2022 at 11:11am and I am, to the minute, 33 years old. I just earned $70, 390 from the launch of my new program. I have $142, 546 in my savings account and just bought myself a new white Tahoe for $54,355 cash for my birthday. I know this because I see the amount in my bank account and I see the spa day I am treating myself to on my birthday as well as driving to that appointment in my white Tahoe. I hear the celebration music playing while I excitedly share this birthday gift with my online community. I hear my mom excited and happy about my success. I feel fucking ELATED, so proud of myself for coming so far even when things got so insanely hard. I am not worried about little things and people in the past, I am on a whole new vibration now. I feel accomplished and ready to continue expanding my career and up-levelling my life! I'm so happy and excited for this next year of my life! I always knew I would be here by this time. I achieved this because I am extremely resourceful, intelligent, tenacious, hard working, great at content creation and attracting my soul clients, focused and most importantly; I never stopped believing in myself and my abilities.

"To be happy with yourself in the present moment while maintaining a dream of your future is a grand recipe for manifestation. When you feel so whole that you no longer care whether "it" will happen, that's when amazing things materialize before your eyes."— Joe Dispenza

WOMB MEDICINE

As humans we've become disconnected not only from Spirit but also from our bodies. As women we've become disconnected from our intuition and the wisdom of our wombs. We live in societies that don't honour the different phases of our cycle, that teach us we must push through our bleed and perform as normal through our Temples' monthly changes. We feel such a deep connection with the moon because we too have sacred phases, this is the beauty of the feminine. In some tribes I've visited, the women wear a different symbol on them specifically for when they're bleeding, and this acts as a sign for those in the community to give her extra care that week. If she's carrying something heavy, someone will help. If she's cooking, someone will offer to take her place so she can rest. During our bleed it's said that we are more connected to our psychic powers and the energies of others. This is a very auspicious and spiritual time for us that should be honoured as such.

When we learn how to honour and listen to our womb space then we begin to truly learn what we want from this life. Chinese medicine refers to the womb as "Zi Gong" which translates to "Palace of the Child". It truly is a Holy, mysterious, miraculous palace. It is the only place where life is created, nourished and birthed from. Because of this, it's an infinite resource of creative power that we can tap into and learn how to grow our dreams from. This is where our most potent creative energy lays, not only when giving birth. This is how we become magnetic manifestors! You can also tune into this area of the body if you don't have a physical womb, in men the belly is also seen as a powerful energetic space in many ancient traditions. The area of our naval is especially important as it was once where our lifeline existed, the umbilical cord. In Chinese acupuncture this energy point is called CV 8 Shenque; Spirit Gate.

If you're confused about something, ask your womb (or where your connection to your mother's womb once existed). It has a great deal of wisdom and guidance when you learn how to hear Her. If this topic interests you I'd recommend reading the book

Wisdom of the Womb as an introduction into womb medicine and healing. Remember, our bodies are very intelligent, even beyond our own understanding. This space deserves our love and attention. It holds the codes of the universe and our ancestors within.

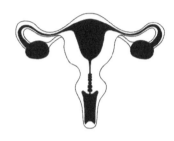

WOMB PRACTICE

Lay down with your back against the earth and bend your knees. Firstly, relax your jaw. Our jaws are attached to our wombs, hips and yonis, if they are tense it's likely our jaws will be tense as well. Notice how often you're tightening your jaw throughout the day.

Become comfortable with being audible. Our vocals are also linked to our sacred yonis (just google vocal cords compared to the pelvic floor or uterus, they're almost identical!) When we release sound we relax our wombs and allow more creative energy to flow within and outside of ourselves.

Place your hands in a triangle shape with your pointer and thumbs touching one another then place over your womb space. At first, don't do anything. Don't have expectations. Just listen. Feel. Open to what your body and womb are asking for. You may not receive any message the first time and that's okay. Just simply be with yourself for at least 10-15 minutes. Journal afterwards any feelings, visuals or memories that may have come up. In *Wisdom of the Womb* they suggest listening for the name of your womb. When I did this the name Lilith arrived loudly and clearly. I never knew the story of Lilith from the bible at that time, but if you do it's quite incredible this is the name that came through! Again have no expectations, just listen as the nonjudgmental witness.

When you feel a little more reacquainted with the energy flowing in this area, honour what your womb is asking for. Your Temple has the wisdom to know exactly what it wants and needs. Perhaps you need to shake, dance, scream... or maybe you just need to stay still and send compassion to these parts of you that you might have ignored for some time.

This exercise came intuitively to me in my womb practice.

As you lay down envision Earth's welcoming, nourishing, healing Motherly energy holding and surrounding you. Feel your connection. Envision roots growing down to the earth from all the parts of you that are touching the ground below. See them move to the core of the earth where her energy is potent and the pulse of your womb synchronizes to the womb of the earth. When we feel out of touch from ourselves this is the natural rhythm we have become disconnected from. Feel your connection to Her and all of the elements. Know that you are a sacred woman.

Repeat out loud, "I am a sacred woman. I attune to the rhythm of the elements. I take back my power." Know that you are safe to embody and own your power, sweet sister. Repeat, "I am safe. I am held. I am exactly where I am supposed to be."

Envision your roots absorbing all of her healing Divine Feminine energy moving up into your physical and energetic bodies. Perhaps it appears as a certain colour. Envision this energy and colour filling up your womb space, circling and growing with healing Shakti frequency. See it filling up the entire room or space around you... the community, the city, the world. Remember your connection to all that is.

Breathe all of this energy into your womb. Repeat again and again, "I am a sacred woman. I attune to the rhythm of the elements. I take back my power."

Allow any noise to come out that desires to. Don't worry about how you sound. Make it weird! Invite your womb to express through sound, to release any energies you're ready to let go of now. Be loud. View the sound traveling from your womb through the solar plexus and heart chakras then out of the mouth, like a vehicle carrying the energies you're ready to release. Do this for at least a few minutes.

Stay still in silence if it feels good for you and breathe into your womb for a few more minutes as the nonjudgmental, loving witness to whatever arises. Not attaching to anything, only honouring and releasing. When you're done have a glass of water and bow your head down to the earth in gratitude and humility. When I practice this small act of surrender it reminds me to have trust in something greater and that my worries are so tiny compared to the big picture. The earth is always holding us and is here for us to come back to whenever we need guidance and healing.

Know that whatever comes up for you while reconnecting to your womb or yoni is perfect just as it is. Again, if you don't have a physical womb or yoni, replace this with what suits you best, we aren't attaching too much to what we see as these are energies from within. Be gentle and compassionate with yourself in the process. Everyone's path is different and many of us are carrying years and years worth of trauma and pain within these spaces, even from past generations or lifetimes. Know that you can heal yourself and reclaim your power, but it most likely wont happen overnight. If the memories or emotions that come up become overwhelming for you, talk to a loved one or a professional. This is powerful universal energy that we're working with, having a support system when needed is important. Remember to journal your experiences.

YOUR MAGNIFICENT, MIRACULOUS TEMPLE

One of the not so wonderful experiences of being human in today's day and age is the idea that we are not enough. It's so silly when you really think of it, isn't it? If you feel this way know that you are not alone. To this day, working with thousands of incredible humans around the world, I have yet to meet one who doesn't struggle with feelings of unworthiness. Again, we live in a society that profits off of our self doubt and disconnect from our true, Radiant Essence, so this is to be expected. As I shared, I struggled with a lot of dis-eases and destructive patterns growing up with zero self love or feelings of personal worth.

I can't stress how important it is on this path of empowerment to get comfortable with your Temple and learn how to love and accept it. This is an act of rebellion in our society! Rebel, sister. Show the world that you have the power and strength to go against what others push onto you, when you know deep within it's not aligned with your own truth and Inner Knowing.

Imagine a world where we all looked exactly the same? How boring would that be? Learn to celebrate the things that make you *you*, on all levels.

Begin by treating your body like a Temple. Feed it nourishing, high vibrational foods from the earth. Personally I've been plant-based for 18 years and when I made the transition is when I began to deeply love myself and view the world around me with more compassion. Going vegan was the catalyst to my spiritual awakening. It's difficult to raise our energetic vibration while consuming animal flesh that's heavy with the low vibrations of an animal that didn't want to die. Their flesh holds fear, pain, suffering and trauma. I'm not here to convince you, but I will encourage you to do more research on the benefits of a plant diet for yourself, the planet and the collective consciousness. I invite you to be present and meditate with your food to feel its energy before consuming, then noticing how it feels within your body. Do what feels the best and most expansive for you, always.

Be discerning with those you allow into your personal space and Temple. No wonder I had troubles respecting and loving myself when I was allowing those who didn't into my life and intimate space. Others will treat us how we allow them to, choose to be treated as an Empress and nothing less. This will take patience, but it's worth it for your mental and physical wellbeing. Learn how to play with that passionate energy within yourself on your own, I promise it can be a lot of fun!

Pray to your food before consuming it. Thank the earth for nourishing you. Eating is the one thing we do multiple times every single day, make it a sacred ritual and your whole life will transform. Prioritize your self care. Prioritize your connection to the elements and earth. Through this connection we remember our power and innate ability to heal ourselves.

A PRAYER TO OUR FOOD AND MOTHER EARTH

I repeat this prayer before each meal.

[Borrowed from my book *The Glowing Goddess Nutrition Guide.*]

Pachamama

Mama Gaia

Mother Earth

Shakti Ma

Our caregiving, nourisher, protector, Mother,

lover, destroyer, creator.

Thank you for gifting us with this meal.

Thank you to those who worked to plant, grow, care for and

prepare this food, everyone who played a part in

bringing it in front of us now.

Thank you for the seeds, the plants, the water, the insects,

the soil and the sun.

May we always treat you with the same care and

unconditional love, Sacred Mother, as you show us.

May this food bring nutrients to our bodies and fuel

to our souls. May it allow us to thrive and embody

our highest selves, for the good of all.

We pray that all beings will have food in front of

them today. May all beings be happy, free, loved and fed.

Thank you.

Thank you.

Thank you.

THE POWER OF HOLDING YOUR VISION

Visualization for me has been one of the greatest tools in manifesting a life beyond my wildest dreams. I believe that in a similar way to how we can remember our past self and speak to her, as we do with inner child healing, we can also tap into our future self and talk to her. I have conversations with my future self all of the time. She tells me what I need to focus on, what or who I need to release and any action steps I need to take to align with my highest path.

I'll often visualize meeting with my future self, or sometimes I embody that I'm already her. As I meditate I imagine my spirit leaving my current body and moving into my future body. I am then meditating in my future surroundings and tapping into my future thoughts; what I did that day, how I'm feeling, what type of things I'll be wondering and dreaming of in that future moment.

Clarity is power babe, you need to know where you want to go in order to get there. Remember, you need to be able to order it up to the Universe confidently and calmly. This comes with focus and a clear vision. Believe and know it is already yours.

Visualize it. Order it. Claim it as yours. Embody it. Own it.

WAYS TO VISUALIZE YOUR FUTURE

- Create a vision board

- Keep photos of what you're calling in where you'll see them often; on your phone, laptop, walls, in a picture frame, etc.

- Get crystal clear on your goals for the near and far future.

- Bring awareness to and release limiting beliefs that are holding you back. You are worthy of all your wildest dreams, and then some!

- Find future self meditations online and learn how to communicate with your future self.

- Have affirmation and reminders on your phone to remind you it is already yours.

- Try hypnosis.

- Watch your language. Don't say, "I want to do that..." or "I'm trying to call that in..." Instead affirm, "That is already mine." Or further, "I am so grateful for ____ being mine! Thank you Universe!" Speak in present tense.

- Celebrate it before it's yours and get on the vibration of already having it. (Just envision my little chi-weenie doing her happy dance!)

- Always, always, expect miracles.

Empress Tip:

Don't leave out any details and dream BIG. I'll keep repeating this because it's important: the subconscious loves specificity. Don't hold back or play small when it comes to your dreams. Open up space for the "Im-possible". Open up space for miracles. Sometimes we have a limited vantage and it helps to leave a little room for the Universe to surprise you. Always go bigger babe.

I believe every woman in the world deserves
to feel sexy, to live wildly,
to not be shamed for her different phases, emotions and changes.
To live a big, bold, and colourful life!
To be as loud as she wants
and to rest and recharge when the time calls for it.
I believe she should be able to run naked in nature,
talk to flowers and chase the wind.
I believe she should have time to rest and reflect during her bleed
and be deeply honoured at this time.
I believe it is her birthright to be
abundant, prosperous and powerful.
I believe she deserves the safe space to be herself,
unapologetically.
I believe every woman deserves to feel drop dead gorgeous and
to love every single inch of her body.
To transcend comparison and competition between others
and rise in love and compassion.
I believe every single woman deserves to feel she is worthy,
that she is more than enough,
that there was never a time she wasn't
and never will be a time she isn't.
She is perfect just as she is.
To know that her authenticity
and perceived 'flaws'
are where her true beauty
is found.
I believe every woman deserves to live
a life beyond her wildest
dreams.

SELF REFLECTION

1. When you speak the abundance affirmations out loud, what feelings come up for you? Where do these feelings come from?

2. Do you feel truly worthy of calling in all that you desire? What might be standing in your way?

3. What limiting beliefs around your self worth, career, and money have you held onto since childhood? What steps can you take today to release these stories?

4. Write down ten things you've accomplished in your life that you're proud of. What did you have to do to accomplish these things? What personal qualities did you have to focus on and grow?

5. If your confidence and self worth increased by 10%, how would your life be different?

6. What does financial freedom look like to you? How does it feel within your body?

7. List all of the ways you trust and believe in yourself. If the list is limited, pretend you're already there and own it!

8. How is this world full of unlimited resources and abundance? List all of the ways.

9. If the frequency of abundance were a person, what would they look like? How would they act, talk, walk, and be in the world?

10. Write in detail a day in your life when you have complete financial freedom and are living aligned to your Highest Empress Frequency.

Queen of Wands

CODE IV: I OWN ALL PARTS OF MYSELF AND WEAR MY PAST AS ARMOUR. I DECIDE WHO I AM AND THE WORLD ADJUSTS.

THE QUEEN OF WANDS: THE MYSTICAL BADDIE
ELEMENT: FIRE

Spend a moment looking at her image and you'll feel the Queen of Wand's fire. I refer to this Queen as the Mystical Baddie because she is fierce, liberated and doesn't care what anyone else thinks. She lives life by her own terms and shines her authentic self unapologetically. The Queen of Wands has been through the dark night of the soul. She's hit rock bottom, and she's used the experiences that led her there as building blocks to create the life beyond her wildest dreams. She is the Phoenix risen from the ashes of the past and she is unstoppable. She doesn't require validation from anything or anyone outside of herself.

I don't watch a lot of TV shows, but once I watched a season of Game of Thrones just to know what all the hype was about. In one of the episodes, Tyrion Lannister says to Jon Snow (the 'bastard'), "Let me give you some advice, bastard. Never forget what you are, the rest of the world will not. Wear it like armour, and it can never be used to hurt you." Those words really hit me.

Tyrion's statement shares the idea that when we fully own the most difficult to accept parts of ourselves, the *shadows*, we're liberated from suffering due to the judgment of others. Does this mean we have to wear our past for all to see and tell the world about everything we have been through and overcome? No. (Although I'll admit, pretty much all of my dirty laundry and experiences are posted online for the world to see, but that route isn't for everyone!) Not everyone deserves to hear our story or experience our depths.

As women on this planet it's totally natural to care about what others think. We want to be loved and accepted into the tribe. This dates back to ancient times. We don't need to continue hiding who we are and what we've been through in order to be accepted, this has actually caused more separation. We are at a time where we must share and speak our personal stories so that we can heal and rewrite the collective stories together. We are at a time where authenticity and showing up as yourself requires much more courage than pushing away your feelings or attempting to appear like everyone else. Be like the Queen of Wands and let your freak flag fly, baby! Know that no one else on this entire planet has experienced what you have or perceives this world exactly the way that you do, and that is your power.

Your unique story is your power.

The Queen of Wands has fiercely dived into all aspects of herself, the light and the darkness, and in the process has mastered self awareness. She knows exactly who she is, honours where she's come from and knows where she's going. According to *Mirror of the Soul*, her leopard used to be a black panther and has undergone transformation with her, its black spots represent the darkness of the past. Her crown still has the nails from the crown of thorns, honouring the suffering and humiliation she experienced in order to become who she is today. Can you relate at all?

The parts of our path that we are most ashamed or afraid of, the parts that are truly difficult to overcome, are where our medicine may be residing. This is often where the deepest, most sacred lessons for our soul's growth exist. From our hardships and challenges we become who we came here to be. What we do with our pain determines our character. We are what we do with our pain.

For a moment, close your eyes and envision yourself in your dream marriage. You have three children (just imagining here!) with your partner, you're excelling in your career and everything seems to be going great. You're happy. You're content. You have the life you always dreamed of. One day you come home to your partner with their belongings packed and they tell you that they're leaving you. They've fallen in love with their secretary who is many years younger than you, and bought a house in Mexico on the beach with them. Overnight, you're left with the kids alone, a big empty house, and no partner. The rug has been ripped from underneath you.

Over the following years, you allow the trauma of that experience to affect your life profoundly. You replay the moment of coming home to your partner leaving you. You replay thoughts of them with their secretary in Mexico while you slave away taking care of the children. You let yourself go and stop caring for yourself the way you used to. You become overweight. You compare yourself to younger women. You obsess over trying to hide your true age. You lose trust in finding love and seclude yourself, focusing all the love you have on your children.

Eventually your children leave to University and you're alone. You've let that experience define you. You've replayed it again and again and can't even imagine remarrying. You see families at school gatherings and feel pity for yourself that it couldn't have been your life. Every time you talk to your ex it hurts. Because you replay the past, your subconscious views it as the present, so you're literally reliving it over and over again. Your subconscious doesn't know the difference between past, present or future. You live in victimhood and believe that only bad things happen to you, that you don't deserve real love.

Now envision the exact same scenario, only you didn't allow this situation to define you or your self worth. You look back on your partner leaving you as the best thing that ever happened to you! It shook up and redirected your life for the better. It showed you who your partner truly was and you know that you deserve so much more than that. You took the kids and started a new life for yourself. You didn't live in the past but allowed it to make you stronger and to know exactly what you value and want from a partner. You took the extra energy you had being single and started your own business that's now very successful. It wasn't easy. You took the time to mourn the loss of your old life, but you didn't allow it to close your heart. You are now in the most amazing partnership you could've ever imagined, far more fulfilling than your first marriage! You look back on the situation without emotional attachment, for you know it was only the Universe rerouting your path so you could move onto something even better. You choose to remember your ex-husband for all the beautiful memories you shared and don't allow his energy to affect you when you're in contact.

Which woman would you decide to be? Look back on the trauma or obstacles you've faced in your life, have you been reliving situations from your past? Have you allowed stories to run in the back of your mind based on events that have happened? Have you identified with or based your worth on the way others have treated you? We have the choice to either allow our past to define us, or to rebuild us. We have the choice to relive our pain or to open right now, today, to something even better.

Let's look at the saying, *pulled the rug out from under you.* I've felt just like that more than once in my life. Let's look at it from a new angle babe. If you pull a rug out fast enough, the item (or hypothetically, you) will still be standing as you were before it was moved. Could you still dare to stand tall, even when reality as you knew it has disappeared before your eyes? Could you still find an inner stillness and strength even through the collapse of everything you thought you knew, believed in and identified with? I believe spiritual awakening happens when you can witness "rock bottom" as the first stepping stone to your new chapter. When you allow your life to destruct. When you let everything go without too much fight, even when God knows you want to. You softly witness the ashes of what was your life and you decide to take that first step. You don't know where it's going, but you know it's a new chapter full of exciting mystery and endless possibilities.

You trust, even when you can't see, that there's something more waiting for you ahead.

Transform the perceived blocks into building blocks for the life of your dreams. If you've gone through great struggle, congratulations! You now have the tools to design a better, more aligned version of your life. You are never too old and it is never too late to rebirth yourself and start over again. Stop standing in your own way. Stop believing the limiting stories from society and hurt people you may have crossed paths with. You are epic and you can do whatever you believe you can do, I promise!

Fiercely show up and demand what you deserve from life, no one else is going to do it for you. Save your own self. Know that you have the Universe supporting and holding you. You are co-creating your reality with the same forces that created this entire world. The options are limitless and your power is immeasurable.

Don't be afraid to step into the fire and witness life as you know it burn to ashes. The flames of transformation can be scary when you don't know what's waiting on the other end. You know it's going to hurt and wonder, "Is the pain of burning really worth it?" I've leaped into those flames heart first and I can tell you from experience, when the smoke clears and you find the strength to rise again, there is always something better waiting. Your dreams are worth the discomfort and even the momentary suffering. The risk of living the life you are meant for, is always worth the mountain you may have to climb to get there. The Queen of Wands reminds us that we are stronger than we could ever imagine.

The life you deserve is worth the pain of releasing and rebirthing. The strength and self knowledge you gain in the process, is worth stepping into the unknown. This life is meant to be lived and you aren't meant to spend it numbing yourself from your potential and inner power. You aren't meant to spend it comparing yourself to others and playing small. You will rise again, as many times as you need to. When you choose the brave path of feeling it all, you will embody all that you came here to be.

Let your fire burn baby. You are meant for greatness. Know that you chose your past, it didn't choose you. You control your inner state. You control your destiny. Your soul chose the experiences you've been through because you knew you were strong enough to endure them. And not only endure them, but thrive from them. You knew that you would use it all as a catalyst to the life of your wildest dreams. You knew you would rise again.

The suit of wands represents creative energy and new ideas. Creative energy is the same as sexual energy. During Code IV in Empowered Empress Mystery School, we dive into our unique sexual expression and learn how to play with and embody this sacred energy. Within you, whether you've embraced her yet or not, is the bad bitch archetype. Sexual energy isn't wrong, it's actually the most sacred thing in this existence. Without it we wouldn't exist! It's just another form of life force energy that we've labeled and attached so many ideas to. We've spent thousands of years having this life force energy shamed sister, and now we're reclaiming it.

"Perhaps the Western mind has become fixated on the sexual dimension of Tantra simply because we have undergone 2,000 years of sexual repression. Certain influential individuals created a spiritual world view which repressed women and consequently diminished our potential of having direct access to the divine through sexual ecstasy.

Tertullian, one of the founding fathers of orthodox Christianity, said: 'Women are the gate by which the demon enters.' Tantra is not fixated on sex but simply accepts and honours it as our primordial energy." — Kindred Spirit Magazine, Issue 93

In Code I we became comfortable with our personal pleasure and began honouring what feels best and most expansive for us. Now, let's go a little deeper. Let's play with the shadows. Every single human on this earth has a shadow self, or rather, parts of ourselves that we don't want to shine out into the world or share with others. I'm going to introduce you to mine soon! Before we begin, take a moment to reflect on the parts of yourself that you may be ashamed of or feel shy to share with others. Can you challenge yourself to love these parts just as equally as the parts you happily shine out into the world?

Shame, in some form, is held within us all. We're born onto this planet, no one is perfect or even knows what's going on, and we carry the heaviness of guilt, shame and self doubt. We feel as if we're somehow inadequate and everyone else has this great adventure of life figured out except us. While it's silly when we truly reflect on it because we are all equally God's children, guilt and shame are very real and can control our lives if we don't bring awareness to these feelings within.

In *Love and Awakening*, John Welwood gives the analogy of a castle to represent our inner reality. Imagine having a magnificent castle with long hallways and hundreds of gorgeous rooms. Each room represents a different aspect of your being that equally makes up the whole. As a child you began to explore every room of your castle, with full acceptance and love. Everything was so exciting, mysterious and beautiful to you. You were proud of your magnificent castle and every room in it. You couldn't wait to share this immaculate space with others.

Eventually you welcome visitors. To your surprise, a visitor tells you that your room is imperfect, perhaps even something to be ashamed of. They suggest that you lock the door to that room if you want to have a good life, and even be a good person. You're embarrassed that you didn't realize this room was so wrong. As time goes by more visitors come and judge the rooms you were once so proud of. Eventually you close and lock more doors, afraid of further judgment and shame.

Over time you've closed many doors to your castle based on the expectations of those in your life, society, religion, and even strangers on the internet. When the doors close on certain parts of your magnificent castle for long enough, you even forget they ever existed. Which rooms have you locked away and neglected in your own being? What parts of your self and your past do you feel shame around?

I think of myself at seventeen years old. As I'm staying in my hometown for the first time in over a decade while I finish this book, many memories have felt fresh in my heart. I distinctly remember that year being one of the hardest of my life. Seventeen year old Krystal put her worth in her sexuality, searched for validation outside of herself, tried to appear and act how she thought others (and society) wanted her to, put high value on her physical appearance and material possessions, didn't know what self love meant, struggled with depression, social anxiety, substance abuse, self-harm, bulimia, body dysmorphia, suicidal thoughts and didn't believe she was worthy of anything good in life.

Whew, that was a lot and there's still more to it. I don't want to say it was all challenging, but my teen years were definitely tough and didn't come with many uplifting memories. I was attempting to numb my fear and pain from childhood. It felt like I was being chased by my demons and searching for any way to escape them. I didn't have a support system back then as we moved around too often to create solid friendships. One of my greatest intentions behind all that I do, including the books that I write, is to remind others they aren't alone, to avoid how I felt during those years of my journey.

I was the perfect product of a society that told me I wasn't enough. That I had to buy things and live a certain way in order to be happy. That I had to be anything but my beautiful, unique self. I look back at my photos during that time and they all look the same. I'm hiding behind a ton of makeup, fake smile and very clenched jaw. How many of us have similar stories? Of course, in today's society (and in history) it's so common. I'm not sharing this to imply that part of my journey was wrong in any way, but to honour where I came from and the different versions of me that got me to where I am today.

I share this part of me with you because it was just before I woke up to the world around me and began questioning everything, while believing nothing. It was my first Divine storm, where everything rose to the surface and I was left with the decision to either continue numbing my reality or face it head on. As you can most likely guess, I chose the latter. That was a sacred version of me before I leaped into the unknown and began traveling the world alone searching for answers. And guess what?

I found them.

Here's the secret of the Universe, really. You could stop this book right here and now after the following information. The information that took me traveling to hundreds of churches, temples, countries and tribes around the world to truly understand. It's the most important thing I will ever and could ever share with you. Okay, ready for it?

Here it is...

You, my Darling,

are perfect exactly as you are right now, in this moment.

You are enough.

There has never been a time in your life when you haven't been enough, and there never will be.

You are worthy.

You are so fucking worthy!

You are worthy of the life you desire, you are worthy of the sex, career, relationships, lifestyle, success, and love that you desire.

No one has ever been more worthy than you,

and no one ever will be.

You are a beautiful, sensual, sexual

Empress, Goddess, Queen, Priestess, Wild Woman, Sister,

you are ALL of the things in your own unique expression.

YOU have the power to create universes within your soul.

Every single thing you are seeking is already within, just waiting to be awakened and embodied.

It is only the environment and the stories you've formulated based on external factors that have led you to forget this.

You have the world, the Universe, in the palm of your hand, and no one is stopping you from being all that you came here to be,

except maybe yourself.

Okay, my job here is done!

If only it were that easy, right? Go back and read those words a few more times. Don't just scan over them, really sit with them. Observe how they feel within you. I know you've all heard (as I just also shared) that everything you are seeking is within. And it's true. I traveled the world searching for everything outside of myself, only to find myself seven years in laughing hysterically alone on a white sand beach in Australia, meditating to sunrise, when the depth of that truth profoundly hit me. When I realized all the traveling and seeking had given me priceless experiences, but the true fulfillment, truth and love I'd been searching for was within me the whole time, like a treasure chest waiting to be discovered.

Even when you come into the knowing of these statements to be true, it's still not enough. Knowing is the first step. Releasing comes next. Having the courage to go against societal standards and forge your own path comes next. This is the true rebellion, my love, learning how to love ourselves no matter what anyone else in this world says. Allowing the layers of our old selves to burn so that our True Essence can appear, then learning how to embody and fiercely own it.

I accept all parts of my journey because if any were spared I might not be here sharing this with you or following the path that I am now. I know that it's my calling to help empower others through my own experiences. I also know that if you shared these sacred truths with seventeen year old Krystal, my journey to self love and a life beyond my wildest dreams would have been much shorter. It wouldn't have taken me long to realize my worth once it was brought into my awareness that I could be more than what my environment and the people around me told me I could be. But, we can't force anyone's eyes to open, we can't force a flower to blossom early, and we can't control the timing of our lives, as much as we might try to at times.

I'm grateful to be here now to share this wisdom with you and perhaps make your journey to the love and life you deserve a quicker one than mine. The truth is this, my love; you don't need to become anything you aren't in this moment already. You only need to release the layers of conditioning that have made you believe you aren't enough. The flames of transformation are the flames of releasing, burning all that you thought you were in order to reveal and come back to your True Self. This is your Great Remembrance.

Do you remember when you were a little child? Did you play dress up? Did you ever pretend you were a princess? Did you love Disney movies? A lot of us like to say Disney movies ruined it for us, leading us to believe we are meant for a happily ever after and giving us unattainable expectations. While I don't agree with the part where a handsome prince has to come and save us, as we are more than fully capable of saving ourselves (another big lesson I had to figure out for myself), I do believe there's a reason we loved those magical, glittery tales so much.

We loved them because we believed them. We believed anything and everything was possible for us. We believed that we were meant to be magical, radiant Princesses, Queens, Witches and Magicians. To live abundantly and dance through life singing and spreading our beautiful unique Divine Feminine Essence everywhere we go. This is an inner knowing all children are born with; the knowing that we are meant for Greatness. We aren't meant to play small but to shine, to use our voices, to love, to dream, to be free! Do you ever remember worrying what others thought of you when you dressed up in a way that lit you up from within? Of course not! We have so much we can learn from children, and the inner child within each of us.

Eventually over time this knowing and inner magic began to dim. We stopped imagining who we could be, where we could go and what incredible things we could do along the way, and started settling for what was in front of us. Our environment (like most public schooling systems) didn't encourage our unique creative genius. Over time we began to believe that we aren't worthy, that we aren't magical Queens fully capable of giving ourselves every single thing we dream of and desire.

If this book landed in your hands (or on your screen) it's because you are a woman, a soul, who wants more. Again, there's nothing wrong with wanting more from your life than what's in front of you. You are a soul who knows she is here for Greatness, who knows she doesn't need to settle in any area of her life, who knows she has the power to create any life she wishes for herself. How do I know this? Because our inner knowing guides us to the lessons our souls need in order to blossom.

On some level, you already know everything I've been sharing with you, that's why you are here and manifested these words into your life. It's your choice, and only yours, what you choose to do with this wisdom from here on.

This is your sacred reminder and I won't stop reminding you of it; you are already everything that you are seeking. This process of self growth, of becoming, is one of unbecoming. Within you already exists the most brilliant, radiant, confident, sexual and sensual Divine Being you aim to be. Within you already exists the Queen of Wands and every other archetype mentioned, only waiting to be activated and embodied. Every version of you that might seem so far away at times, already exists within.

When the veils of illusion dissolve, all that's left is love.

OM GAM GANAPATAYE NAMAHA

In Hinduism, Ganesha is the God often recommended to work with before others. This is because he's the one who removes obstacles from our lives. He's the one who releases the layers that are holding us back from knowing our True Selves.

What some forget to acknowledge is that he's also the one who places obstacles in our way. The remover and giver of sacred challenges. If it wasn't for the difficult times we wouldn't be able to grow into who we came here to be. We've been programmed to believe that the darkness and the challenges are *bad,* when really they are gifts and opportunities for us to discover our power and truth.

If you'd like to begin working with the energy of Ganesha, chanting his mantra every day for 108 time is a great place to begin. Perform this mantra meditation with a mala necklace, most come with 108 beads. Mantras can be very powerful to use and I recommend also doing research on these sacred vibrations and their history. I believe it's very important to understand the origin of the tools we use so that we can honour them, the culture they originated from and understand how they can empower our lives as well as the lives of others.

The mantra is*: Om Gam Ganapataye Namaha.*

GRATITUDE TIMELINE PRACTICE

Draw a timeline from the day of your birth until the present moment. Include all major obstacles. You may want to write these out first then add to the timeline. These moments could be a physical injury, the death of a loved one, physical or emotional abuse, trauma, your first heartbreak, first betrayal, first mistake, financial obstacles, or anything else that comes up for you. Take your time with this, your timeline may become quite full and that's great! The more you've written down, the more opportunities you've had to grow.

When you've completed your timeline, spend a few moments taking it all in. Look at all the sacred challenges you've overcome and grown stronger from! You should be so proud of yourself.

Now, on a separate piece of paper, write out why you're grateful for each obstacle and at least one thing you learned from it. You may be surprised with what you discover!

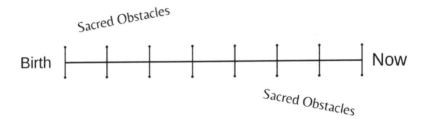

AFFIRMATIONS
TO REMEMBER WHO THE FUCK YOU
(ALREADY) ARE

Repeat the following out loud a minimum of three times, say it in front of the mirror. Memorize it. Put reminders in your phone. With the constant stimulation we receive each day that tells our subconscious we aren't enough, it's important to constantly affirm and remind ourselves of these sacred truths.

I am more than worthy and always have been.

My presence is enough.

I am the source of my own pleasure and power.

I am my own guru.

I am my own lover.

I am my own Universe.

I am my own before I am anyone else's.

I decide my worth.

I decide who I am and the rest of the world can adjust.

I decide the standard of life I live.

I have the power to call in all that I desire and make my dreams a reality.

I am the Divine Feminine embodied in my own
unique, brilliant, messy, gorgeous way.

I stand proudly and fully in who I am.

I am responsible for the state of my life and
I choose to make it epic!

A life of abundance, love, joy, and pleasure is my birthright.

I reclaim my throne and fiercely rule my Empire
with courage, love and compassion.

I am a powerful, sovereign, determined, Graceful Empress.

Let's jump from seventeen year old Krystal to twenty-two year old Krystal, an international exotic dancer who is in the midst of finding her voice, owning her unique gifts, and stepping into her power, but still has a long way to go. After leaving a very abusive relationship, I went from an extremely shy, timid girl who couldn't look others in the eye, to a strong, clearly spoken, confident woman within a year.

I understand there's a lot of shame around the sex industry. As I've shared, in Tantra (and in my opinion one of the most important aspects) we release shame around ourselves, what we consider to be *wrong* and accept that we are perfectly imperfect humans. This is my story, and I wouldn't change it for the world. My hope for you is that you can feel the same about your past too.

I'm going to spare you the details of how I got to that lifestyle, but I will say it was a very fundamental part of getting me to where I am today. What I will share is this; if you told me back then that one day in the future I'd be writing a book and sharing that I was a stripper in "Asia's Las Vegas" (Macau) and then around the world, I would never have believed you. I was living a double life and I got really good at it. My evenings were spent working in nightclubs having cash thrown at me and my days were spent visiting Buddhist lectures and Hindu ashrams as a "nice" yoga teacher.

And you want to know something? No one I met in either environments were better, more "pure," more deserving, or more "sinful" than the other. We are all souls in these precious human suits, playing out our roles for a temporary time. No one is better or worse. We are all just doing our best with the tools and experiences we've been given. This is Tantra; knowing that all aspects of this adventure we call life are Divine. Every. Single. Part. We are each on our own unique path; awakening, learning and unlearning in our own way, in our own sacred timing.

An Empowered Empress doesn't judge herself or others for where they are or where they were on their path. She knows that every single step is sacred and holy in its own unique way. The key is that we are always learning from those steps, even when we may not be aware of it. To be empowered is to take ownership for our lives and not fall into victimhood, believing that life is happening to us rather that for us. It's knowing that we are not defined by our current circumstances but what we choose to do with them.

Fast-forward to Krystal at twenty-five, no longer a dancer and managed to keep those experiences a complete secret for years. The truth is, I'm an absolutely terrible liar. I get it from my mom, she can't lie if her life depended on it. When I went back to my hometown and someone directly asked me, "Krystal, are you in the sex industry?" I immediately started shaking and turned red hot while shouting about ten times higher than my regular voice, "NO!" (And yes people asked this, I'm from a place where everyone is in everyone else's business.)

While the experience of the industry was overall empowering for me; I learned how to present myself confidently, talk to men, set strong boundaries and create a new life for myself with the money I earned, it was eating at me that I had to remain quiet about it. The shame around these parts of myself didn't feel authentic. I felt ashamed about something that I didn't personally believe was shameful. I knew something had to change. I knew I had to fall in love with my shadow self and stop caring what others might think of her.

My shadow self is Kat. That was my dancing name and the name I went by during that time in my life. No one knew me as Krystal, this is how I kept my two lives separate. I always saw Kat as wrong, bad, naughty, dirty, sinful, wild and... FUN. She was my most expressed self that couldn't be shown in regular society. She was the fierce, sexual part of me that had been shamed my entire life. She was the part of me that wanted to be celebrated, and the more I pushed her down the more she wanted to come forth and play.

When I went back home that year I made a decision, I was going to fall in love with Kat. Not only fall in love with her, but I was going to celebrate her. I began openly telling my friends from high school about my experience as a dancer. I quickly realized that when you don't care about something and don't shame it, others naturally don't either. No one seemed to judge me or have an issue about it once I wasn't trying so hard to hide it.

This goes back to Tyrion's words. When we wear our past proudly no one can hurt us with it. When we fully accept all parts of ourselves no one can hurt us by calling us names, judging or putting us down for not fitting into their perceived idea of how we should be living our lives.

Beyond just owning Kat, I wrote her love letters. I wrote that I was sorry for treating her so poorly over the years, for judging her, for shaming her and for thinking she wasn't worthy to shine out into the world. Most importantly, I told her I was sorry for not telling her that I loved her sooner.

At that time I was working as a yoga teacher and no longer dancing so my income was much lower, but I put some money aside and had a four foot painting created by an artist friend, Jason Skeldon, of Kat. I told myself one day when I have a home (hopefully that day comes!) I'll hang it up over my fireplace. How's that for celebrating?

I'm not saying you need to get a painting done of your shadow self (although I promise it's very empowering!) but I am encouraging you to celebrate and fall in love with all parts of you. The beauty of being cyclical by nature is that we aren't just one way all of the time. We aren't one dimensional. Like the moon we are constantly changing and evolving through our phases, and each and every version of ourselves deserves to be loved equally.

Self love isn't about loving yourself when things are going smoothly and you're completely happy in life. It's about diving deep into the depths of *you* and discovering exactly who you are... fears, doubts, desires, fantasies, embarrassing moments, messy insecurities and experiences you don't want others to know about, and falling madly in love with it all. To me, that's the true "living my best life".

You deserve to be loved for who you are, even on your darkest days. You deserve someone who will stick around through thick and thin, never judging and only loving. You can be that person for yourself, because at the end of the day, it's always going to be you.

Every single relationship and situation in your life is a direct reflection of the love you have for yourself. Accepting your shadow bits, the parts of yourself you hide from the world, doesn't mean you have to start telling everyone about them the way I did. It just means that you accept yourself so deeply that you no longer care what others think. You have freed yourself. And not only do you deserve to be loved fully... **you deserve to feel free.**

Release the veils of illusion and accept that your essence is eternal Love and Bliss. Want to live a life of pleasure, expansion and freedom? Make love to life itself. Have the greatest romance you could ever imagine: with existence. Observe and admire the life moving through your body. Open up to how good it truly feels.

We live on a blue planet that circles around a ball of fire next to a moon that moves the sea, and you don't believe in miracles? -Anonymous

Life is pretty damn magical, huh? It's so easy to get caught up in every day stresses and routines that we forget just how incredible it is to simply exist. We live in a society that rewards us for *doing* rather than *being*, but we are human *beings*. We thrive when we are in balance with our masculine and feminine energies. When we honour when it's time for us to take action and when it's time to rest.

An Empowered Empress is in a love affair with life. She's devoted to herself and the Divine, as herself. This doesn't mean that she doesn't move through different emotions and seasons of her life, but that she welcomes all of the changes and phases in with as much love and grace as she can. She knows that like the moon, her phases are temporary and contain their own blessings and miracles. She doesn't view parts of her past as wrong, they just simply are. She's released the emotions attached to past circumstances in a healthy way, so they no longer come up when those memories may appear. And if they do, she knows how to release them rather than allow them to control her actions.

While some spiritual paths aim to disconnect from the body and the senses in order to reach higher states of consciousness, Tantra opens fully to life and satiates the senses. Your awareness then goes fully into the body and expands to the subtle realms using the physical as a pathway, rather than by rejecting it. This is what makes Tantra different from most other spiritual practices.

There's so much to be grateful for and so many gifts to the senses in each and every moment. Again, how much pleasure you experience and how much love you bring into your days is always your own choice.

You are already enlightened, pretending not to be.

Shiva and Shakti are the Eternal Lovers, they represent everything outside and within us. These Divine energies are in an unending love play that manifests as the world we know.

One day Shakti danced around her Beloved Shiva and asked him,

"My love, how would you like me to appear today? Who would you like me to be?"

As eternal energies they are able to become any face and form.

Shakti is all of the faces of the Goddess, just as each of us are.

After thinking for a moment Shiva replied,

"I would like to you to show up as Kali."

Shakti was surprised. "Of all the forms I could be, beautiful Lakshmi or Devoted Parvati, why would you choose Kali? The dark image that so many find to be unattractive, messy and even scary?"

Shiva replied, "Because my love, that is when you are your most expressed self. That is when you are most free."

Our darkness is where our authentic beauty resides, if we only dare to embody Her with absolute acceptance, courage and radical liberation.

THE GREATEST LOVE AFFAIR

Take a deep breath in.

Do you feel that?

Within your very being is everything that ever was and

everything that will ever be.

Stop playing small.

You are built of ever-moving, ever-flowing, ever-dancing, ever-shining particles of light and love.

A Divine manifestation of

Energy and Consciousness,

Earth and Sky

Shiva and Shakti,

the Eternal Lovers..

forever colliding and separating,

uniting and parting.

loving and longing.

all within and around you.

Your existence is as big as the mountains,

the trees, the stars and the seas.

Everything you are seeking is within.

Empress, everything you are seeking is within.

No greater Truth has been told.

No greater love could unfold.

Stop searching outside of yourself

YOU are love.

You are perfection.

You. Are. Everything.

The Universe desired you.

The Universe conjured you up.

So it could experience life through your unique reality.

You have never needed to change.

You have never needed to be anything except who you are right here and now.

When the veils of illusion dissolve, all that's left is love.

You are exactly who and where you're meant to be.

So fall in love with the life moving through you.

Open up to the infinite pleasures of the senses.

Discover the ecstasy this very moment holds.

Remember where you came from.

Then,

Everything you touch

everything you experience

everything you see

becomes the greatest

love story that could ever be.

HOW TO MAKE LOVE TO LIFE

- Practice seeing the Divine in everything. As Ram Dass said, "Treat everyone you meet as if they are God in drag." Can you see the Divine in every face? Every tree? Every cloud? Can you feel the same life force energy in you as the people and things around you? Can you feel it in Nature? Close your eyes and try. Practice this while walking down the street. Take it all in as different expressions of Source. Be enraptured by all of existence.

- Practice morning gratitude. Before you even open your eyes begin listing all that you're grateful for. At the end of the day, journal all of the little miracles and beauty in your day. Make it your mission to find as many as possible.

- Celebrate! Dance, sing, rejoice. You are fucking ALIVE, what you can experience here is limitless and that is worth a daily dance celebration.

- Practice a dynamic meditation or ecstatic dance with others.

- Practice opening the senses fully while you eat, walk, shower, etc. Smell your food before eating, feel the texture of your clothes glide against your fingertips before changing, imagine you can touch and feel music while you move to it.

- Wake up and ask: *How can I celebrate life today? How can I make love to life? How does life choose to celebrate itself through my vessel today?* Envision yourself making love to life during the day ahead. How does that look?

Close your eyes, sit with your breath and fall in love with the life moving through you. Send love to the breath moving in and out. Send love to the senses, send love and healing to everything around you. Envision the sounds, tastes, feelings, images and colours around you as little vibrations of love and pleasure coming through your being. Tantra doesn't escape this moment, but fully experiences it. This is how the "mundane" becomes extraordinary.

How ALIVE can you feel right now?

SELF REFLECTION

1. Name your shadow self, describe what she's like and write an acceptance and love letter to her.

2. What are the parts of you that you hide away and what are the parts of you that you shine proudly out into the world? Write them down and compare. Could you love and accept all of these parts of you equally?

3. How does your environment and the people in your life affect you? Do they support the person you are becoming?

4. How judged do you feel on a daily basis? How often do you worry about what others might think?

5. What's one thing that you know you need to do in order to fully accept yourself, that you have been avoiding?

6. What feelings and emotions do you associate with your shadow self? Do you label these feelings as good or bad?

7. Look back on your intentions at the start of this journey. How can you nourish these more moving forward?

It is the love and trust within your heart that magnetizes you to the richness of life's limitless possibilities.

Trust enough to let it all go.

Love enough to do so with grace.

Trust enough to be patient.

Love enough to open space for what is on its way.

Sweet soul,

You deserve better than to settle.

You deserve better than to wonder,

"What if?"

Gift yourself with the possibility

of having it

all.

CODE V:
I PLAY WITHIN THE MYSTICAL REALMS AND ALIGN WITH MY HIGHEST EMPRESS FREQUENCY.

THE PRIESTESS: THE SACRED SORCERESS

You may already be acquainted with the Priestess archetype and her subtle yet powerful presence in some way. She's the spiritual essence within each of us. The Divine Feminine power that lays within, waiting to be rediscovered and activated. In our world today, we put a lot of value on the physical, when the Spirit is where the true treasures of life exist. The Priestess is connected to the cosmos, the spiritual realms and higher states of consciousness. She's somewhat mysterious, as she's beyond this physical world and beyond our logical reasoning.

When we learn to call her forth and activate her energy from within, we receive a deep sense of belonging and purpose. We remember our place in the world as a sacred, spiritual being. You'll have to look closely at her image on the Thoth Tarot to see her, this is because she dances in the subtle realms. She appears to be flowing and free, reminding us of our own ever-changing, natural essence. We aren't meant to stay the same, we are cyclical beings. When we remember this and learn how to release attachments as gracefully as we can our lives become a lot smoother. When we learn how to choose the path of less resistance life can become really delicious.

The Priestess reminds us to have trust in a greater plan for ourselves than we can even imagine. Oftentimes we become so attached to outcomes or the idea of how things *should be* that we miss out on the magic being offered in its place. The Sacred Sorceress within each of us reminds us of the magic, the mystery, and the mystical, in this life and beyond.

I used to strongly attach to fantasies and dreams for the future as I'm very idealistic by nature. What I've come to realize through my experiences of trail and error, broken hearts, disappointments and crushed dreams, is that sometimes the fantasy is actually better than the reality. Sometimes right here and now is better than anything you could actually experience when you've formed expectations. Sometimes it's all right here already, if you dare to honestly look within.

If we attach too much to our dreams outside of the now, we might miss the blessings being offered to us that are more aligned with our highest purpose and pleasure than we could have imagined. Learn how to surrender and trust that the Universe is always working in your favour, no matter how much at times it might appear differently. Learn to pause, look around, and open to the infinite pleasure and abundance being offered to you already.

The Priestess reminds us of the beauty found in letting go. Often our greatest suffering is only from the ego attempting to grasp onto what we know cannot last. I envision it as though I'm floating down a river. At first I'm enjoying it and having fun, but then I begin to panic as I realize I don't know where it's going. I try to swim against stream and burn myself out. I try to hold onto branches and rocks with all of my strength, but eventually have to let go. My panic and fear grows the more I attempt to hold on.

Finally, I lay back and breathe. I stop trying to control the flow of my journey and allow it to guide me into the great unknown. I liberate myself from my own struggle. As I relax, I realize the sun is beaming down on me magnificently, birds are flying above and the river isn't so scary after all. I see it from a totally new perspective, and it's all perfect. I trust. I surrender. I flow. The journey now becomes pleasurable, and even a whole lot of fun!

The Priestess also connects us to our intuition and psychic powers. In our Empowered Empress training, during our Priestess week we learn about the Tarot and Astrology as tools for self empowerment. These tools can be used for divination, to predict our futures, but I personally enjoy using them as navigation systems back to our true selves. The title of the book for the Thoth Tarot

that I've referenced, *Mirror of the Soul,* is exactly what I believe
these cards to be. They reflect parts of our soul that might not have
been brought into our awareness otherwise. They make the uncon-
scious conscious. Without tools like this or other spiritual practices, we may end up walking through our lives on autopilot and
not truly *living* at all.

**We must know ourselves deeply in order to love our-
selves deeply.**

As I often say, the first step to self love is self discovery. This is
also the first step to self empowerment. I'm deeply grateful for
these tools that have brought me deeper into my-self. I've already
mentioned the Tarot and how it has helped me. I'll also mention
Astrology, Human Design, Akashic records, past life regression,
personality tests, and visiting psychics. I share more on some of
these topics in our school.

If any call out to you and you're unfamiliar with what they are, just
follow your intuition and jump online to explore. Of course there
are endless tools to discover yourself, that's just some that I used
in my life. Isn't it such an interesting topic, discovering the self?
We are magnificent, unique imprints of the same Source. Life is so
cool.

In my perspective I view Astrology and other maps of our souls
(such as human design) as clues from our souls before manifesting
into this reality. Clues that we can use to understand what we need
to do, and what we must avoid if possible, in this lifetime. It's kind
of like a love note from the soul before it came into physical manifestation. How else could our limitless spirit contact our future,
limited human mind? I believe we chose the exact time of birth,
our exact parents and this exact manifestation with deep purpose
and intention. Whether you agree with my view on this or not is
totally up to you, but either way these tools can be great for discovering new parts of yourself you might not have otherwise!

As I shared at the start of this book, holding a Tarot deck is like
having a whole Universe in the palm of your hands. Before I discovered them I used to say that we were born into this world with

no guidebook, now I see them as our cosmic guides and Astrology as our soul's blueprint. I studied sciences in University and always had a strong logical mind, so I pushed away these tools for many years, but after seeing them work and be wildly accurate again and again, I had to surrender and trust that there's some magic at play and begin sharing them with my community. The results have been incredible.

Call upon the Priestess when you're ready to dive into the mystery of the cosmos and your soul. When you're ready to come back to Mother Nature and the rhythms of life and the elements. Since she plays in the subtle realms, she reminds us of our connection to all that exists. She reminds us of our connection to the trees, animals, ocean and rivers. Sit in Nature and call upon the Priestess, she will guide you to what you need in order to align to your HEF. Because the plants, animals, stones and waters are much older than us, they have sacred lessons and stories to share, if we simply remain silent long enough to listen. Remember Empress, you are so much more than the physical. You are an infinite, limitless, manifestation of the Divine Feminine, and no one is exactly like you. I think that's something worth celebrating, don't you?

The Priestess is the Moon Goddess, represented by Isis. When we reconnect to the phases of the Moon we reconnect to the cycles of our own Temples. Whether you physically bleed or not, we are all affected by Grandmother Moon and her powerful, mysterious presence. In my book *Awakening the Goddess* I share some simple New Moon and Full Moon ceremonies. I'll share some Moon magic in this chapter with you again. I encourage you to sit with the Moon and intuitively hold your own rituals. You can do this any time of the month, but the New and Full Moons are especially potent times for manifesting, releasing and rebirthing.

I deeply believe that if everyone could sit alone in a room with their own self, and find love and acceptance for what they discover there, the whole world would change. That's the work humanity needs. When we all come back to Spirit and remember this connection is when the collective will heal.

PRIORITIZE SPIRIT

An Empress cannot find her power outside of herself. The moment you seek validation, worth or pleasure externally, you're putting yourself in the position to experience unnecessary suffering. Not that this is a terrible thing, as we've already discussed, suffering is at times very important for our growth. Still, we can learn how to avoid excess pain and insecurities, which many of us are currently experiencing on our planet. We each deserve a life of joy, fulfillment, great sex, incredible food, and healing, soul deep connections.

Why is there so much suffering? Because we have become out of touch with Spirit. We've become disconnected from the True Self and our inner knowing. We've become distracted from the fact that all we need to do to be happy is come back to ourselves. Spirit is available to us in every moment.

God, Divine, Shiva, Source, Spirit, Allah, Goddess, whichever name you prefer to use, it's the life force running through you (and the one you should be madly in love with after the previous codes!) As discussed in Code III, spirituality is often seen as separate from worldly, material life. In Tantra we enjoy all of life. Nothing is rejected, everything is accepted. We now know that we can be, and deserve to be, abundant on all levels; spiritually, financially, physically, emotionally and materially! This life is meant to be enjoyed (and celebrated!) It is our birthright to enjoy it on all levels and in all realms.

With that being said, the pull outward might always be stronger than the pull inward, because it is right in front of us, and we live in a society that values the physical. It's easier (and sexier) to desire a shiny new gem necklace or commit to the gym when you're starting to notice your booty getting results than it is to commit to that which we can't see, or even understand.

This is why daily, consistent practice (*sadhana*) of coming back to Spirit is so important. Eventually we begin to crave going inward because that's where the true treasures and pleasures are found. We may not be able to see it, but we can feel it more deeply than anything solely in the physical. Aim to be more aware in your practice and throughout your day. How deeply can you experience this moment?

In yoga we learn that there are five layers to the self, or *koshas*. The Anamaya Kosha is the physical body, the Pranamaya Kosha is the energy body, the Manomaya Kosha is the mind and emotions, the Vijnanamaya Kosha is the wisdom body and the Anandamaya Kosha is the Bliss body. When I share that the Priestess plays in the realms of the subtle bodies, I'm referring to the bodies (koshas) beyond the physical, or Anamaya Kosha.

Many spiritual paths view identification with the physical as the root cause of all suffering. When you identify with something outside of yourself it's said that you've lost your soul. When you've lost your soul you go through life in a type of hypnosis or sleep. To awaken from this state one must distance themselves from their thoughts, emotions and actions, and simply watch as the non-judgmental, loving witness. Behind all movement (Shakti) is a stillness (Shiva). Remember your centre, remember the calmness behind it all.

WAYS TO CONNECT TO SPIRIT

- Goddess *puja* (worship)

- Sensual *puja* (worship/gratitude of the sacred senses)

- Mantra and Yantra

- Prayer and surrender

- Affirmations

- Visualization

- Self worship/admiration

- Creating an altar

- Meditation

- Breathwork *(pranayama)*

- Yoga

- Going into Nature, connecting to the rhythms of Mother Earth and the elements

- Transfiguration: practice seeing the Divine in all

- Connecting deeply to your food and eating fresh, high vibe foods from the earth

- Embracing your humanness as Divine: emotions, feelings, all of it! Open to higher states right here and now, rather than searching for it outside of yourself

- Play: Create, dance, express! Get into a creative flow and become a clear channel for Shakti to express herself through

- Have conversations with your higher self, angels, spiritual guides, etc. Open to hearing and receiving messages from the spirit realms

- Connect with a guru, shaman, or spiritual teacher who can guide you deeply into your-self

- Practice being in awe of life, open to the beauty of Nature, embrace this moment as deeply as possible. Search for the Divine Feminine Beauty in everything

- Sit in sacred sisterhood and community. Open to learning, sharing and growing with others. Practice seeing Shakti in your own eyes and in your sisters'. Always be a student to life.

- Trust and connect to your Intuition, your higher Self (your highness/HEF!) over the limited ego

- Search for beauty, magic and miracles in everything. Always.

PRAYER TO SPIRIT

GREAT SPIRIT,

I surrender. I trust. I open my heart.

Please allow me to come back to my True Nature,

to remember my Divine Essence and

sacred connection to all that is .

Please allow me to release the things that aren't serving my highest
good here, for the good of all.

Give me the strength to stand tall in my

truth, to share and speak it from my heart,

to not be blinded by the illusions of the material.

Please allow me to deeply love all parts of myself and others,
Mother Earth, and our relatives;

the humans, animals, plants, stones, and all beings.

May I live in peace with my surroundings.

May I see with clarity exactly what I will stand for

and not stand for. And always honour both.

May I step lightly on this earth,

and may my time here be an expression of

Divine Feminine Love and Compassion.

I surrender. I trust. I open my heart.

RULE YOUR PLEASURE

At the start of this journey we dove into our pleasure and learned how we can reclaim it and welcome even more into our lives. The journey of empowerment, to me, is a journey of deep, mind-blowing, consistent, pleasure. Why, you ask? You can read all the self help books and hire all the life coaches in the world, but if you haven't reclaimed your pleasure and your Divine Feminine Essence, you're missing the key to everlasting fulfilment. Your body will still be craving the feeling of being *alive* and *turned on*.

As I've shared, when you prioritize your pleasure and dive deeply into the sensory gifts each moment holds, you awaken your connection to Spirit. Take it from me babe, I've visited spiritual and religious churches, temples, ashrams, monasteries, tribes, and more while traveling the world over the past decade. I'm deeply grateful for the experiences I had and the amazing teachers I've met, but even when I became a yogi I felt there was something missing. My daily practice felt dull so I started to neglect it. I couldn't attend yoga classes because half way through I was so bored I would often sneak out the back. I felt guilty that my discipline wasn't stronger.

My search for what was missing from my practice finally ended when I met an awakened, sensual, Divinely Embodied teacher and her essence showed me what I was missing: pleasure and play.

The feminine wants to be expressed, seen, pleased and AWAKENED.

When we experience pleasure and aliveness, we release the feel good hormones; dopamine, oxytocin, serotonin and endorphins. These are the sacred hormones of love, connection, pleasure and joy! And they can become addicting. I started to add more play into my yoga practice, creating *Sensual Shakti Yoga* (now *Sensual Body Love Yoga*) in 2016. At first I didn't want to create my own form of yoga as I wasn't sure if that would be respecting the tradition, but my HEF kept telling me to... you guessed it, do what feels good and expansive for me!

My classes are full of juicy, feminine, sensual, flowing yoga and movements based on listening intuitively to the body and moving however feels best for you in the moment, rather than predetermined asanas. Now we also practice naked yoga in classes to form a deeper connection to our Temples. Most of yoga and meditation is masculine. Masculine empties the mind and has an end goal, while the feminine opens the heart and flows freely.

The difference between traditional yoga and Tantra is that in yoga, it's often believed that one must follow a lifetime or lifetimes of laid out practices in order to reach liberation. Osho says that in Tantra, it's like pouring an ice bucket over one's head while they're sleeping. This is how you awaken and reach liberation through Tantra; immediately. In my experience, pleasure has been the ice bucket to awaken and shake up my soul in my practices.

Once I added more pleasure and play to my practice, and my life, that's when I finally felt that I could create the empire of my dreams, call in the man of my dreams, and magnetize all of my deepest desires. This is being in the feminine flow. If you're having troubles committing to a practice or healthy new hobby, figure out how you can add more pleasure to it. Once your body begins associating those feel good hormones with your new daily regime, you'll have no problem making time for it!

Osho also said, "Practice kills life." He encouraged others to live fully in the moment and as spontaneously as possible. Of course, that's not always possible for those who have schedules and deadlines. I do agree with this approach and believe we should live as freely as we possibly can, rather than pushing ourselves to do things that don't light our soul on fire. For me, it's been fun to play with this approach when I have the freedom to do so, and also discover new ways to feel free in my routine as well.

You are enough.

In fact, you are so much MORE than enough.

You are MAGNIFICENT.

You are Powerful.

You are special. You are unique.

Everything you have been given, you are worthy of having.

You are worthy of being here, of being in your body,

of being on this earth.

You are worthy of living a life that utterly excites,

pleases and fulfills you!

You are worthy of healthy, deep, authentic,

meaningful relationships.

You are worthy of time for self-care.

You are worthy of financial abundance.

You are worthy of treating yourself. You are worthy of relaxing.

You are worthy of sharing your voice and speaking your needs.

You are worthy of being confident and feeling sexy.

You are worthy of feeling valued.

You are worthy of TRUE, deep, unapologetic self love.

You are worthy because you are a child of Mother. Of the Divine.

You ARE the Divine.

Know this to be true, and live in accordance with your Greatness.

MOON RITUALS

Begin to pay attention to which phases fall on which calendar days, perhaps have a reminder in your phone. There are some great apps that share the moon phases and planetary movements. Once you begin to get in tune with the Moon cycles, you begin to connect deeply with the cosmos and nature. Choosing to tap into the energy of the moon can add an element of beauty, mystery, and flow to life. This brings awareness to other cycles and rhythms within your own body, mind and spirit. Try these rituals for each new moon and full moon to begin reconnecting and aligning deeply with the moon. Personally, I like to plan the rituals and take a relaxing Goddess bath beforehand.

NEW MOON:

1. The new moon is the perfect time to assess what needs to change in your life and to create new intentions to follow. What do you wish to manifest over this next month?

2. Find a sacred space, being outside under the moon if possible is best.

3. Smudge the area with your intentions in mind.

4. Set up an altar with all of your favourite sacred items. Lay your crystals to recharge, use items that connect you with nature: a feather, flower or seashell, for example.

5. Make a fire in this sacred space. Light candles if an outdoor fire isn't possible. Fire represents transformation, change and new beginnings.

6. Prepare beforehand a paper with all your desires. What would you like to manifest? What would you like to ask the Universe for? You might want to begin the paper with something like, *I accept the following into my life for my highest good and the highest good of all.*

7. Now you may want to begin by offering gratitude to the Earth and Moon, and acknowledge the elements. Speak your intentions for this new moon. Speak your desires. Include a poem, song or instrument that helps to set the energy. If you are performing this ritual with others allow them to speak their intentions.

8. Burn the paper with your intentions. Fire also represents action, know that these wishes will be put into action as you watch it burn. You may wish to meditate or write in a journal how you will put these desires into action within the following month.

9. During the following weeks be aware of your intentions and the actions you're taking to embody them. Have them written around your home to be reminded.

FULL MOON:

The Full Moon is a time to release that which no longer serves your highest purpose; what you no longer need in your life or an aspect of yourself that you have outgrown. The moon energy is powerful and intense. This surge enables you to take aligned action, especially in regard to the New Moon intentions you may have created a couple weeks prior. The full moon is a time to let go of anything that has been weighing you down or holding you back from living the life of your dreams. Do you feel heavy? Is there any pain, resentment, jealousy or anger you may be holding on to? It's time to release all that no longer serves your highest path. Repeat steps 1-4 of the New Moon ritual.

1. Prepare a paper beforehand with everything you'd like to release from your life written on it. Meditate on your fears, small or big, and write them down. Think of any current attachments you may have, any expectations, blockages or anything getting in the way of you reaching your most sacred goals.

2. Again, acknowledge the elements, the Earth and Moon, and your Divine guides of choice. Ask them to help you lose the following from your life in order to live your highest good. Speak all of the things you are ready to release. Some examples may be: Fear of change, comparing yourself to others, holding on to past lovers, seeking approval from others, releasing a job or relationship, old limiting beliefs, clinging onto things outside of yourself, unhealthy expectations, the need to control, jealousy, resentment from the past, worries of the future, the belief you are not good enough, childhood wounds, financial worries. Of course, you'll intuitively know what needs to go.

3. Follow with a poem, song or instrument that helps to set the energy. If you are performing this ritual with others now allow them to also share what they wish to release from their own lives.

4. You may wish to burn the paper, rip it into pieces, or send it down streaming water, watching it float away. I always choose recycle paper for my journals.

5. Thank your guides and Higher Self for helping you along your Divine path by giving you strength to recognize that which is no longer serving you and the courage to release it.

6. During the following weeks be aware of any fears or things you'd like to release popping up, and gracefully let it go. Record these experiences in your journal if you'd like.

BLOOD MAGIC

As explained previously, we've been disconnected from our wombs, pussies, and bodies for some time. Because of this, for those who bleed monthly, we've also become disconnected from our own sacred blood. To some, the idea of this blood being sacred grosses them out or even triggers them. Don't worry, I used to be like that too. As I became deeply connected to my Temple and honoured it for all that it does for me, this time of the month became incredibly special.

I remember I used to apologize to my boyfriends when I was younger for getting my *period* (I personally no longer prefer to use this word) as though it were a negative thing. I apologized because we couldn't have sex. Like it was some terrible, shameful thing! Now the partners I choose love this time of the month and treat it as very sacred with me. They are not appalled by my beautiful blood, but admire it. It makes me woman. A woman who can birth life, and there isn't much more sacred and magical than that. While I like to spend time alone to reflect and relax during my moon time, I do find it to be a very special and potent time for lovemaking, something I previously wouldn't have considered.

If this is new to you, I'm inviting you now to rewrite the stories you have around your monthly bleed. Reflect on your introduction to your bleed. Was it treated as sacred? (Note: If you don't bleed this can still apply to you. How does the monthly bleed of others make you feel? It's important for all of us to reflect and rewrite these stories for the healing of the collective sacred feminine). Whether you bleed or not, how was your introduction into puberty? How did you and those around you view the changes happening to your body?

It's said that this time of the month is the time we have the most powerful psychic and spiritual powers. In some cultures the women are spent away from others during this time. In some religions women aren't allowed into Holy places at this time. A patriarchal society is afraid of a woman in her full power, which is why miraculous gifts like our sacred blood have been pushed away and made to feel shameful. When you really think about it, it's crazy, right? To shame something so incredible and mysterious? We've attached so many negative beliefs around what is so natural.

Becoming a woman and bleeding for your first time used to be a time of initiation and ceremony. It was seen as a monthly renewal; death and rebirth. A reminder of our connection to something bigger than ourselves. A mysterious time aligned with the moon and an opportunity to release the old and manifest the new, every 28 or so days.

Do you usually bleed around a specific moon phase? Do you bleed at the same time as your mother, sister or friends you spend a lot of time around? That's so sacred and again the intelligence of our bodies reminding us of our connection and how we are meant to be in sacred sisterhood.

Our blood is a gift. It is a miracle. It is our medicine. It is our Truth. It is potent with the codes and mysteries of this wild, wonderful existence.

WAYS TO CONNECT TO YOUR BLOOD

- Reconnect with the womb and yoni using the prior practices.

- If it feels good for you, use a yoni egg when you aren't bleeding and practice yoni steaming.

- Create a Moon Time Basket and keep your favourite items for this time of the month in it. Keep a special journal (I use a red journal and pen) to record your thoughts and feelings at that time.

- Pay attention to how you feel throughout the month and reflect if there are any repeating themes on certain moon days.

- Practice free, natural bleeding. Place a towel down when possible rather than using products that block the flow.

- Look at your blood, don't shy away from it. Become familiar and comfortable with it.

- Track your cycle on a phone app and take note of your emotions and physical wellness on different days of the month.

- Keep your blood. Have a ritual of offering it into the earth, connecting to Shakti (Earth) on even deeper levels.

- Create a Womb Cocoon for this time: a space you can be in peaceful solitude. Women used to spend this time away from their families and in sacred sisterhood. (I highly recommend the book *The Red Tent*.)

- Wear the colour red and decorate your home or altar with it. This represents Shakti and blood.

- Anoint yourself with your blood. You might have seen images of women wearing their blood on their faces (it's also said to be great for the skin, which I personally practice often), set your intentions and place your blood on your third eye, heart, or anywhere else you feel called to. Let this be your initiation into blood magic and mysteries. Let this heal your connection to the most sacred parts of your Temple.

- Make love. This can be a very powerful time to connect with your partner, if you have one. Otherwise make love to yourself! Notice if and how your pleasure is enhanced at this time.

- Yoni gaze while bleeding and see the beauty and sacredness in this miracle.

"A Woman in harmony with her spirit is like a river flowing. She goes where she will without pretence and arrives at her destination prepared to be herself and only herself. "

— Maya Angelou

SELF REFLECTION

1. How connected do you feel to Spirit? Do you feel/believe that you are the Divine embodied?

2. What are your spiritual beliefs, if you have any? Explain in detail.

3. What are your favourite paths to self discovery? What new tools are you going to try moving forward?

4. Look up your natal chart online if you haven't already. What have you learned from your unique planetary placements? What surprised you? What did you already know about yourself?

5. Take a personality test online. Just Google and see what comes up then intuitively choose! What did you learn about yourself from this new perspective?

6. If you physically bleed, how comfortable are you with your blood? How will you strengthen this bond moving forward? If you don't bleed, how does this topic make you feel, and why?

7. What spiritual practice are you committing to for the next month and how will you make it pleasurable?

8. Do you feel connected to the moon? Read about the different moon cycles and what they represent. Create your own Moon Ritual. Record how it felt afterwards.

9. Write out your own prayer to your food and Mother Earth. Begin using it before each meal. If you don't want an entire prayer, "Thank you" is also enough.

10. How connected do you currently feel to your intuition and inner knowing? Why do you think this is?

CODE VI:
I RECLAIM MY THRONE AND RULE MY EMPIRE AS A FIERCE FEMININE LEADER.

THE EMPRESS: THE RADIANT RULER

The Empress does not rule the world, she is the world.

We have now journeyed through all four of the Queen Archetypes, into the mystical Priestess, and have finally arrived at our Empowered Empress. The Empress energy is multidimensional and complex. She is many things, just as we are as women. We play out many special roles: sister, mother, leader, friend, lover. The Empress reminds me of Durga, the fierce Hindu Goddess who holds the energy of many Shaktis within.

An Empress is a little different from a Queen as she is a sovereign ruler. The Queen archetype is often seen as a great lover and consort. The Empress often stands alone, and isn't afraid to do so until she is met with an Emperor worthy of standing beside her. She's passionate about building and ruling her Empire. She is here to change the world, for she *is* the world. She's passionate about equality, human and animal rights, environmentalism, and helping shift the world into a more compassionate and loving environment for all.

The Empress has powerful Mother, Earth and Venus energy. She is abundance and beauty embodied. She's her own Universe and looks to no one and nothing outside of herself for validation, pleasure or affirmation. With that being said, the most powerful women are often the most soft. She owns her vulnerability and isn't afraid to be fully authentic. She expresses her emotions and feelings in a respectful, compassionate way. She is fiercely compassionate to herself and others. She is an empath and a sensualist. She wasn't born onto the throne, but had to endure and thrive through a long and deep journey into the depths of herself to arrive there, as we have with our journey through the previous archetypes. The Empress is an embodiment of all the Queens and Priestess qualities integrated and then celebrated. She has reclaimed her power and although self doubts and fears may still arise, she doesn't allow them to affect the trajectory of her life.

The Empress doesn't rule above anyone. She has been on a path of self awareness and awakening for some time. She didn't step into her power overnight. It came with great resilience, clarity, failures, successes, humiliation, trust, truth, and faith. She learned how to be there for herself when no one else was. She didn't expect to be saved, and became her own Heroine instead. She has transitioned from the Princess to Empress. Oftentimes this comes with deep suffering and rebirth.

I know most of you who have read this far will resonate with this initiation. The initiation from Princess energy into Queen/Empress. For me this looked like releasing blame on others for hurting me or influencing my life in what appeared to be a negative way. It required me to let go of my victimhood and take full ownership for my life. Many of us were victims and powerless when we were young. All of us have some form of trauma from childhood. It's natural to feel like a victim when we actually were at one point and had no control over our surroundings, but we take our power back when we realize we now do. When we own the fact that how we live our lives now is our choice, and ours alone.

You have chosen the path of the Empress, perhaps without your awareness. You haven't chosen the path of distracting yourself from the things that happened in your past and pretending they never existed. You, powerful babe, have chosen to wholeheartedly show up. Your soul, as far out as this may seem, desired to go through the difficult times that it did in order to grow and become who you are today. The more I work with others around the world the more I believe this. By now, you've found forgiveness and maybe even some grace within your obstacles so you can move forward and blossom out of the darkness, or perhaps the light.

The Empress, the Royal High-ness, may seem tall up there on her throne, but she is deeply in service to others. She is dripping in self love and pleasure because she knows that in order to serve the best she can, she must fill her cup first. Cleopatra desired more than anything to protect and sustain her people. She was a powerful leader and as rumour has it, was all about personal pleasure and exploration! While we can't believe all of the stories (history tends to create scandals around famous women), it's apparent in the records that she celebrated her sexuality and sensuality, unapologetically.

Sister, we are living at potent times on our planet. We can't continue to pretend that we aren't rapidly moving towards destruction of the Earth or, more likely, destruction of humanity. Collectively, we are not in a healthy state. Whether you choose to bring this into your awareness of not, you're still affected by the collective frequency on our planet. I don't share this to scare you, but to tell you that you are here to be the revolution. The Feminine Revolution. The shift into a New Dawn.

If you've been called into the Empress energy it means you are ready to be a part of this collective rebirth. This Great Awakening that we can't deny is currently taking place. The true Empress doesn't rule to stand taller than anyone else, but to lift others up to stand beside her. Become the leader of your Empire, and lead first by example.

This is the era of feminine leaders. For the past 5000 plus years, patriarchy has ruled our lands and societies. The cultures in history who respected and listened to the feminine were in harmony with Shakti, with Mother Earth. They respected all life forms and flourished as a result. The true feminine leader rules from her heart and not the ego. She rules strongly and softly at the same time. She leads with the collective in mind. This is what will save our species and the generations to come. Our beautiful Mama Earth will always find a way to balance herself over many years. She doesn't need our help, we need hers.

In our final code I invite you, Warrioress, to become a Fierce Feminine Leader of the New Era. This doesn't mean you need to begin teaching like I do or start preaching your truth across social media (but if you feel called to this, please do!) This is a sacred invitation to step back and look at your life from a Higher Perspective and ask yourself: *How can I be of service to others? What impact is my existence currently creating and is this in alignment with the impact I truly desire? How do my greatest goals and dreams also benefit the collective? How can I share my Feminine Essence in a way that empowers and heals others?*

FEMININE LEADERSHIP

"The world will be saved by the western woman." — Dalai Lama

We are all leaders in our own way. Whether you realize it or not, others are paying attention to what you're doing and looking up to you. As you know by now, our societies have been overly masculine for some time. What this looks like is governments fuelled by greed, money, competition, possession, war and prioritizing individual goals over collective healing.

Many ancient cultures have known that we'll be shifting into a more feminine era at this time on Earth. This is the healing we need. This isn't about the feminine overpowering the masculine, but rising up to meet the masculine in sacred balance. It's about bringing more compassion, intuition, emotional intelligence, and respect for Mother Nature and all of her beings, to the collective consciousness.

While it's apparent that many in power have been asking themselves the questions, *How can I make more money? How can I remain in a position of power? How can I use others, and Earth's resources, for profit? How can I make it to the top and succeed?* The Feminine leader asks, *How can I support my community today? How can we grow together? How can we communicate in a way that pushes us all to succeed? How can we show our respect and care for Mother Earth? How can we all win and thrive equally?*

A feminine leader honours her intuition and listens to her inner knowing (HEF) over her logical mind. We use our emotional intelligence to guide us in conversation with others and step out of our individual ego while making important decisions. We don't expect others to be a certain way that suits our own needs, but rather guide them gracefully without expectation. We know that we can't push others to think or be the way we'd like them to and accept them as they are in this moment. We know that everyone's awakening at their own individual pace and trust in Divine Timing.

Know who you are as a feminine leader. How do you want to make others feel in your presence? Lead with compassion. Lead from the heart. Lead your days and your life from a space of unconditional love for all. Dare to create change. Be passionate about uplifting others, because you know that nothing beats the feeling of being in genuine service. Take impeccable care of your Temple and yourself, as you know by raising your own personal vibrations you're raising the collective vibration.

Be the fierce, compassionate, loving leader of your Empire.

That's all it takes. You can share your unique, healing, loving essence with the world in countless ways. Even if you work at a cafe, you can make your presence one that heals others. Pray into each coffee cup, look people in the eyes, smile, compliment them, hold a fundraiser or bring the homeless man across the street a latte on your lunch break.

It's not about what you do, but you how do it. Your actions right now, no matter how small they may feel, create a difference. The difference humanity could use at this time. Never, ever doubt your ability to change the world for the better. Never, ever doubt your ability to change someone else's life just by your warm energy or smile.

How can you bring more Empress energy into your life as a way of personal empowerment and service to the collective?

What exactly does feminine leadership look like to you?

I learned how leadership looks to me specifically once I began holding women's events and retreats. I hadn't realized until then that I still had some major blockages around my own sister wound. The sister wound runs deep and most of us carry it is some form. This manifests into our lives as resentment, pain, jealousy, comparison, feelings of inadequacy, competition, and even rage towards other women. This could be from this lifetime or lifetimes before.

My sister wound revealed itself during one of my first women's only retreats. What this looked like for me was playing small as a teacher and as a sister. I was shying away in front of the women in circle, not speaking as clearly as I'd like to and becoming nervous that they'd judge me, wouldn't accept me, or wouldn't like my teaching style. As a result I wasn't holding space the most powerfully that I knew I could be. Memories of my own sister abusing me verbally and physically, and girls from high school ganging up and hospitalizing me arose between my classes.

I thought to myself, *Wow, here I am holding these events attempting to heal the connection between sisters, and look at my own experience. Who do I think I am?*

I knew I was someone who deeply wanted to heal these parts of myself as well as guide others to do the same. I kept showing up the best I could and continued to work on accepting and loving the parts of me that were afraid to shine out of fear of being attacked for doing so.

I went to a lot of different schools growing up, because I was always the "hot new girl," I was bullied and physically attacked by other girls often. During class I'd hide in the back of the room and tried my best to be invisible. I didn't wear makeup and avoided walking by older guys. I remember trying to take notes in class and my hand constantly shaking uncontrollably out of fear. I'd eat my lunches in the bathroom stalls so no one could bother me. I learned how to hide my beauty, my gifts and my light so I wouldn't upset anyone.

It wasn't until my own retreats that I realized there was a part of me that still saw other women as scary and malicious. The women who come to my retreats have been the most incredible and kind souls, yet here I was becoming triggered from my past and playing small as a leader. I think the world of the women and humans who come to my events. I see the radiant beauty within each of them and feel honoured to witness their presence, their inspiring vulnerability, and a glimpse into their sacred, unique journey.

It took me a few more retreats and sitting in vulnerable circle witnessing their own stories to realize that they didn't see what I saw. I realized that we all have our own insecurities, guilt, shame and feelings of inadequacy. I realized all the women who had hurt me throughout my life had done it out of their own internal hurt. Hurt people hurt people.

I began to feel safe around women for the first time as I came deeper into the realization that they aren't there to hurt me, but to heal with me. They weren't scary anymore and I wasn't a victim. Whether they were a bully growing up or on the receiving end like I was, we were there together to support one another and rewrite our personal stories into more empowering beliefs. This is what the world needs more of; women coming together in sacred circle, honouring whatever comes up, and supporting one another through the healing and growth process.

Honestly, at times I just want to shake the women I work with and scream, *"How can you not see how incredibly Divine and Worthy and Gorgeous and Powerful you are!?"* Of course, I refrain myself and hold space for them to move through their own traumas, insecurities and fears.

I believe I fully stepped into my power as a leader when I let go of the shell that was blocking me from sharing my heart with other women and began to honour my authentic self. I have a massive heart, but when threatened I hide it away. I told myself before each class, *show up as you are and lead from there.* That's all they want. Raw, authentic, imperfect, honest, vulnerable, me. Not some perfect teacher who thinks she has it all figured out. Not someone above them, but a sister who is on the exact same path, perhaps a couple steps ahead, gently encouraging them to hold her hand and walk next to her as sisters.

Unfortunately, my business has also brought me pain from other sister leaders as well. Teachers I hired at the start of my teaching journey made up very strange and hurtful stories about me after I had worked with them. In my reality everything went smoothly and wonderfully, then I'd hear terrible things afterwards. This was part in my fault for making the mistake of hiring and judging others off of their social media while not knowing them personally. I had to learn how to be more discerning in my professional life, and also realized that I wasn't the only one still holding on to the sister wound. These women were also in powerful leadership roles, and still being triggered by my energy in an unhealthy way. I could only feel deep compassion for them, and myself.

The world needs more authentic feminine leaders. We need less of the highlight reels and pretending everything is okay all of the time. We need less pressure to fit in and more value put on individuality and diversity.

In order to share my heart the way I so desired to, I told myself to speak to the women in front of me as if they couldn't see that they're the most perfect, beautiful, exquisite and whole being who ever walked this planet. I got out of my own trauma and began approaching others and my offerings from the deepest and softest places in my heart. You see, I do see the Divine in all. I stopped judging based on exterior qualities when I began traveling and realized that some of the most beautiful souls I'd ever witnessed were women living off of the land without a dollar to their name, a radiant face full of wrinkles and missing teeth. That's right, I discovered beauty I'd never witnessed growing up in the West or around the fashion industry before. The kind of beauty that I can only describe as sunshine in human form.

You can feel that kind of beauty from across a room, and that same beauty is within me and within you my love. How you see me will never be the same as I see myself when I look in the mirror. No matter how beautiful or confident another woman may appear, you can never know what's going on inside of her. This is why it's so important to choose compassion and kindness over competition and judgement. A big part of my mission has been to remind women of that true beauty and radiance within them, their own unique internal sunshine.

It was through learning how to view others beyond just the physical and see the light within us all, that I was able to step into my role as a compassionate leader. I began truly serving from my heart once I discovered how to release my own judgments and create soul to soul connections. Once my heart realized it was safe to open fully in my programs and events, that's when my authentic self shined through and my offerings became my own.

I didn't need to be perfect. As leaders that's not our aim. Our intention is to make others feel like they're powerful leaders as well. This is the Empress frequency; others feel confident and radiant in your presence. The Empress activates the Divine Feminine in others by simply being her powerful, radiant, compassionate and loving self.

What blocks might you have towards other women? How can you show up more embodied in your personal power? How can you lead more from the heart in your own life?

You can take many leadership style quizzes online, but intuitively you'll know what needs to be worked through and what style is best for you. Again, and just like in my own experience, the key is found within your own wounds. We're taking hold of our lives (Empires) babe. We're changing how success, leadership, and power look, because the old way clearly isn't working for us anymore.

This is our time. This is the time of the feminine awakening. How do you choose to show up?

CREATE AND HOLD THE STANDARD

One of my first loves was Scotty, the typical bad boy type who dropped out of school, drank and smoked weed, was in and out of jail and hung around questionable characters (back in high school I had a thing for those types). None of this seemed to bother me. What did bother me was that he was two years younger, and that wasn't the coolest thing for a girl to do back then. Nevertheless, I was obsessed with him. Like, to an unhealthy degree. But we aren't judging here, right? I have always been a hopeful romantic and willing to give love my all, when I was younger and lacked boundaries, that pretty much meant making my partners my whole world.

I believed that in order for someone like him to love someone like me, I had to be like him. I started skipping school, smoking weed even though it made me paranoid and uncomfortable, drinking alcohol, swearing, partying and no longer hanging out with my old friends. I created this entire story that he wouldn't like me if I was a "nice" girl who went to school and preferred her books over partying.

One day Scotty unexpectedly ended things with me because he didn't like who I'd become with him. He was completely unaware that all of these changes weren't by accident, but planned for the purpose of keeping him!

He told me, "When I first met you I thought so highly of you. I thought I could never get a girl like you. You are the Queen bee to me." I responded, "And now? You just think less of me?" I thought his view of me must have been deflated after getting to know who I actually was. "No, not at all. I still think you're the Queen and tried to meet you up there, but I can't do that if I'm dragging you down the way I have been."

And just like that, Scotty gave me my first lesson in holding the standard. I realized that I'd lowered the quality of my life and my values in order to fit into who I thought he wanted me to be. In the end he left me for it! Scotty was ready to rise up, to align with a higher version of himself, and had I stayed in my authentic power we could've possibly grown together.

This lesson applies to all aspects of our lives. Do we want to lower down, denying our true selves to fit into environments, or do we have the courage to walk alone, while holding our personal standards, until life meets us there? Can we be single until the partner we truly desire comes along? Can we be patient to create friendships until those who meet our requirements come into our lives? Can we handle "losing" our jobs, relationships, or other situations because they aren't reaching our standard and aren't in alignment with our highest path? Or will we compromise, make excuses and adjust our boundaries in order to remain comfortable? In order to not be alone? Stand tall in your unique power and truth Empress, and commit to remaining there.

As far as we know, we have this one life. Do you want to spend it playing small, or rising up to all that you can be?

When I started my first business at 19 I had zero confidence in myself and my offerings. If someone told me my services were too expensive I'd adjust the price on the spot! Others would find out about this and all of a sudden I'd be working for a third of the income I expected. When I met a guy I knew wasn't good for me, I'd start adjusting my standards to date him. *I said I wouldn't be with someone who does that... He's really great at that one thing though.. maybe I can just push the other stuff aside and focus on that.* We often do this out of fear of being alone. I spent seven of the past ten years single. It wasn't easy, but I have been patient. I know that holding my standard and having trust that he's out there and coming to me in Divine Timing, is worth it in the long run. I know what I want from a relationship and for my life, and I don't mind waiting.

The Universe listens to what we say *yes* and *no* to. When we're putting energy into the things we don't actually want, we aren't opening space for the things we do want to appear.

I know now that when I set the price for one of my programs, that's the price. Whether five or fifty women show up. The five that do register and don't attempt to get a discount are the ones ready to commit to the program and show up fully. I could continue to date "maybes" or I can continue to work on myself and when the one that's a full body FUCK YES shows up, he'll meet me where I'm at. This is holding the standard; knowing exactly who you are and what you want from life, and not making adjustments when you get lonely, fear others might judge, or things just get tough.

Becoming a Fierce Femme Leader of the New Era requires one very important ingredient; rewriting the stories around sisterhood and reconnecting in powerful community. We are meant to be in tribe. We aren't meant to walk this path alone. We're meant to bleed together. To share about our insecurities and relationship challenges together. To raise our children together. To support and empower one another to live our best lives imaginable. We aren't meant to rise up and stand strong alone but to hold our sisters' hands along the way.

You may have heard of the bug, *comparisonitist*. It's going around.

And it's deadly. It's keeping us playing small. It's hurting us. And it's not allowing us to be who we came here to be. It's everywhere and if you don't pay attention it'll grow and spread. It might even be waiting on your phone now to leap out the moment you click on that little Instagram icon.

The truth is, this has been engrained in our DNA for some time. For a long time in history a woman's worth was based on how she would be as a wife and mother. Quite literally our survival depended on competition between our sisters. My highest intention for creating the Empowered Empress Mystery School and my other feminine trainings is to release the sister wound many of us carry. For me, the relationship with my older sister was one of the most challenging and hurtful I've experienced. As we've learned, our medicine often exists in our deepest pain and trauma, and that's why I personally believe I was led to this work. Again, we teach what we need most ourselves.

We are blessed to live during a time when we can rewrite these stories so the generations of sisters to come might not feel the same pressure as we do now. A massive shift is happening within the feminine. It's an exciting time to be alive babe! The state of our societies and lifestyles are evolving and so should we.

"A sister can be seen as someone who is both ourselves and very much not ourselves - a special kind of double." — Toni Morrison

If you're struggling with the comparison trap whenever you go online, don't worry my love. There are ways to heal this and come back to a space of celebration; celebrating yourself and your incredible sisters.

What we wish for others we wish upon ourselves. If you are judging or rejecting another woman's success, you're telling the Universe that you don't want it for yourself and will remain on that vibration. Celebrate other women!

Any time you catch yourself feeling down from comparing, affirm this: "I am deeply grateful for the women who come into my radar and show me what's possible. I know that if it's possible for them, it's possible for me too! I know that there's enough room for all of us to rise up and shine brilliantly. I am so thankful for those who lead the way and show me what's possible in my own life. I know they might be just a few steps ahead of me on the same path, and that doesn't make anyone better or more worthy. It might just mean that they started before me. I pray for their continued success and happiness in life. I celebrate all of my sisters and by doing so I run on a vibration of the highest love and grace. I welcome in more success, more money, more play, more joy, more sex, more love, more pleasure... into my life and theirs!"

Doesn't that feel so much better than a negative thought towards someone you may not even know, therefore bringing you to a lower vibration? Pay attention to why you judge and where those feelings come from within yourself, rather than projecting them onto someone else. Be grateful for others who act as sacred mirrors to reflect work you may need to do within your own self. Train yourself to replace comparison with celebration and to refocus your energy from putting others down to building yourself up instead. It's all a matter of what you focus on because what you give your energy to will always grow.

In our Mystery School one of the exercises is to go and comment on at least ten women who inspire you's accounts and say, "Thank you for showing me what's possible!" This has become one of our favourite, and most empowering, affirmations.

Honour the younger version of yourself who might have felt inadequate, that sweet young being who deserved to feel beautiful, worthy and whole. In my own experience, growing up I felt like everyone else deserved nice things; nice clothes, nice cars, nice homes, nice families, except for me. I didn't know why, but God had decided I wasn't worthy. I grew up in a low income family, most of my things were from thrift shops or even garbages. This caused a deep soul wound, showing up the first day of school feeling so inadequate, staring at the girls with beautiful clothes and new haircuts (I cut my own hair and actually still do to this day), chatting on their cell phones and driving in their first cars. I lived in a trailer park and used to get my dad to drop me off three blocks from school so no one would see his rusted old van with duct tape along the sides.

I must be very gentle and loving with that version of Krystal and acknowledge she's still within me, and might always be. There are still thing that might trigger that feeling. That feeling I had was valid, and it still is. It was an important part of my journey, a humbling part, if you will. I've learned from these tools that I've shared that there is much to be grateful for from my upbringing, but that doesn't mean it hurt any less at the time.

Discover the root of the feeling that arises when you're judging others or feeling less than, maybe it's not as extreme as mine, but at some point in your life the younger you felt like they weren't enough, and that may be the reason you're comparing yourself today. Honour her, be loving with her, and let her go so you can come back to a higher, more pleasureful vibration.

HOW TO FIND YOUR SOUL SISTERS

- Declare to the Universe that you're going to find your soul sisters. Become clear on the sisters you'd like to call in. What are their values? How do they spend their free time? What type of work do they do in the world? Find women on social media who represent the babes you'd like to call in.

- Unfollow accounts on social media that make you feel worse about yourself or lead you to compare. Follow ones that uplift you and that you'd like to bring into your life. You can even try connecting with them if it feels good!

- Search for events and gatherings in your area (I used to use Meetup.com while traveling). Search for women's circles or hold your own. If you're looking in your area with no luck that probably means other women are as well.

- Connect with online sisterhoods (like my free private Facebook group: Goddess Sisterhood with Krystal Aranyani!) Reach out to other women in the groups and see if any live in your area.

- Don't be discouraged! This path you are walking is rare. To show up and dare to be an empowered babe is rare. That's what makes you so awesome.

Remember to hold the standard in your friendships as well. If you aren't fitting in with others it most likely means that you are here to help create the New Earth, an Earth of empowered sisters who support one another. Trust me, I know what it's like. I grew up in small towns in Northern Canada where women fed off of gossip and competition. I put my intention out to the Universe and eventually found communities of spiritual, powerful, and inspiring Goddesses. They're out there, I promise!

RECLAIM YOUR POWER
(EXERCISE FOR RELEASING
COMPARISON)

Sit in a comfortable position, close the eyes and take several deep breaths into your solar plexus chakra (a couple inches above the belly button). Feel and witness the energy that's in this space for you.

Does it feel empty or weak? Does it feel fiery or strong? Active or still? Feel what is here for you without judgment.

Now, as you continue to breathe into your solar plexus, envision a golden light spreading from this area and around your body, your energetic field and the entire room. With every inhale it's expanding. This is your power, your internal sunshine. Your Radiance.

In this ritual, we are going to fill your energetic field with an incredible sense of your own authentic power.

Together in the power of sisterhood, we reclaim our worth by reclaiming the power we have given away to others.

We have placed our worth in the hands of others around us, and now it's time that we bring our sense of self worth back into our own hands.

No one else can define your worth or your worthiness. YOU define your worth.

Say out loud the situation you've been giving your power away to, the first step is acknowledging it exists as well as *where* it exists in the body.

For example: "I know I have been comparing myself to ____ on Instagram. It hurts in my heart and turns my stomach when this happens. I feel small and inadequate when I compare myself like this. I know that she is just another version of me and she has shown me what's possible in my own life. I won't compare my life to anyone else's because I will never know their personal reality, I only see the highlights."

Then repeat at least three times, "I take back my power from the situations I've been giving it away. I reclaim my power as my own."

Continue to take deep breaths and allow yourself to relax into this space.

Using your intention and your power, call back all the power and all the energy that you have leaked out.

Begin tapping on your solar plexus.

Envision your power coming back and returning to the solar plexus.

Repeat: "Return, return, return. I reclaim my power."

Now that you have reclaimed all of this power, once again envision the golden light surrounding your energetic field. Know that your power is YOURS and when it's around you it can be used as energetic armour. When we are fully in our power and pleasure, nothing can touch us but love.

Feel what it's like to have all of your power present within you, right now.

You have reclaimed it. Witness it. Honour yourself.

All your power has returned in its purest form, clean and cleared.

Breathe that in.

Place a hand on your heart and solar plexus. Breathe into these spaces and feel the connection between the two. The soul and the ego. Personal will and Divine will.

Stay here as long as you'd like. Journal anything that has come up for you. If there's still places in your life you need to bring attention to repeat this again in a few days.

When one woman wins, we all win.

We are of the same fibre, embodied in our

own unique, glorious way.

We are meant to stand together,

to remember our Radiance together,

to rise together.

FORGIVENESS

While you are now busy out in the world creating the Empire of your wildest dreams, you don't have the space to hold onto resentment of any form babe. When we release resentment from the past or pain we're still holding onto, we open up more space to receive. Just as we released parts of ourselves, we should also release any emotions we're still holding onto from our past. Forgiveness is so important so I thought I'd add it in here again as we move to the end of our journey and onto a powerful new chapter of our lives.

Remember, holding on to pain, anger, or resentment from the past doesn't hurt anyone but yourself. By forgiving others we aren't suggesting that what they did was okay. This is for us. This is about releasing any heaviness in your heart or body so that you can live your best life imaginable right here and now.

Write out every person who has hurt you throughout your life. Yes, all of them! Start from childhood and work your way to the present. Spend some time with what you've written. Now place your hands over your heart and repeat, "(Person's name), I love you, I forgive you. I wish you healing and happiness. I love you, I forgive you. I wish you healing and happiness." You may want to also include yourself on that list.

Trust me, I know this process isn't always easy, especially if you've experienced deep trauma from someone in your past. I first started this practice when I had to let go of someone who abused me for years. Every day I practiced this simple exercise and I'd cry. I'd become angry. I'd rage. I didn't want them to be happy, I wanted them to suffer! So I thought. When I came back to my heart and really thought about it, I didn't actually. I wanted them to heal whatever it was that led them to treat me that way. I wanted them to become healthier so they wouldn't treat others the same. I didn't want to see them again, but deep in my heart I did want them to heal.

In that situation it took almost a year to finally say those words out loud and mean them. Let me tell you, once I allowed my heart to fill up with love for someone who had hurt me so profoundly, it was one of the greatest liberations and joys I'd ever experienced in my life.

We aren't meant to hold on to pain, grief or resentment. By learning to fully forgive and release those from our past, all layers of our selves become lighter and healthier. Free your heart and open space to receive all that's coming beauty!

OWN YOUR EMPIRE

Every single thing in your life, from your relationships to your career, to the number in your bank account and the state of your mind, body and spirit... are all caused by you and the choices you have made. Nothing else.

How does that feel to hear? A little triggering? If so, good.

The wounded feminine easily falls into victim mentality, feeling like her circumstances are beyond her control. Remember that we have the power to be whatever and whoever we choose to be in this life! Remember that even if you were a victim at one point in your life, you aren't anymore. This life is YOURS.

Maybe you've forgotten the power that you hold within. That's okay, it happens to all of us sometimes. This is your final reminder of who the fuck you are.

You are a badass, radiant, power-full Empress. You have the power to create Universes within you because you ARE the Universe Herself. You are made up of the cosmos and stardust. You are a living, breathing, loving miracle. If for some reason you didn't get what you want in the past, it's because you were meant for something even better. The only reason you might not have called something even better in yet is because you don't believe it's coming to you! Trust me babe, with a clear vision and a balance between feminine *being* and masculine *doing*, you can create anything that your heart desires. Don't attach your worth to anything outside of yourself; you are unstoppable.

As Empowered Empresses we have now accepted that life is happening for us, not to us. We have taken full ownership for our life situation and circumstances. We now know that we can create any reality we desire.

LOVE HER BUT LEAVE HER.

As mentioned, one of the most special and beautiful things about being a woman (or identifying as one) is that we have so many versions of Shakti within us. We are never stuck one way. We are sacred, cyclical beings just like the Moon.

We have the power and opportunity to be whatever we desire to be in this life. How cool is that? Look back on the history of women and you'll see how far we've come. Often we hear that we aren't treated equally to men and I've personally witnessed this inequality in every single country I've visited (sixty-seven as I write this!)

However, we do have more opportunity than ever in recent history to be the sacred creatrixs of all that we desire. Unfortunately this isn't the case for a lot of women across the world, but as we empower ourselves individually we also empower the collective. It's our responsibility to rise up and use our voices for the women who still cannot.

In Western society we're no longer expected to be stay at home wives, but if we want to that's amazing too! We can be businesswomen, full-time Mothers, healers, witches, CEOs, teachers, digital nomads, YouTubers, yoginis, small business owners, politicians... the list goes on and the options are limitless. Doesn't that feel good?

With all of the endless possibilities in front of you, which roles are you ready to wholeheartedly step into? We've already completed some releasing work in this journey, but the path of letting go of the stories and versions of ourselves that we've held onto is a process. Perhaps this journey has brought up emotions and feelings from your past that have surprised you.

This week is your initiation into Empresshood. This transition shouldn't be taken lightly, it's a very exciting time for you and I'm so honoured to guide you.

There comes a time in every Empress's life when she has to say good bye to the girl she once was in order to sit fully on her throne and embody a new, higher vibration. Again, this doesn't mean those versions of us are wrong, it just means that we have outgrown them.

In my life this meant saying good bye to teenage Krystal, the one who drank alcohol to numb her pain, had no boundaries, and slept with guys who didn't treat her right as an attempt to feel loved and appreciated, even if only for a brief moment. She was the version of me that looked for validation outside of herself, and as much as I loved her, eventually we had to part ways so that I could become who I came to this Earth to be.

To my surprise, this was an extremely painful parting. I brought that version of myself into my awareness and felt her pain and loneliness all over again. I realized I had kept her within me for so many years and she was projecting onto not only my present relationships, but my career and life. I gave her all the love she deserved. I let her know that she wasn't wrong. I let her know that she was always loved, then I said good bye.

Every Empress has her sacred initiation, as I've shared, part of this process is releasing the old so we can create space for the new. We're always opening to the depths of this moment here and now, while keeping a clear vision of the future, and only looking back to remember how far we've come.

What's waiting ahead is always better than what's being left behind because you've grown from the lessons and become stronger every step of the way. You've up-leveled. Therefore whatever you're calling in moving forward will also be an upgrade.

Give yourself permission to open space for all that you can be, and all that you already are deep within. Do one final release of the versions of yourself and stories you are ready to let go of. Be extremely clear and focused at this time. Give your Inner Empress room to reveal herself. Give her space to be big, to be loud, to be fully expressed. Give her room to enter and take reign.

DECLUTTER YOUR LIFE

On the topic of releasing any left over old patterns, behaviours or energies, I believe it's also important to touch on the current state of your castle (home).

As I mentioned, as a full time traveler I don't have too many possessions and I prefer it this way. At this point in my life I've yet to have an actual home, but I'm currently working on making the transition! For many years I only owned two suitcases, so when I'd find something I loved I'd ask myself if it was worth giving up an item I already had for. If so, I'd then keep the new item and give away the old item.

I believe that practicing minimalism and owning less possessions is a wonderful choice for ourselves and the environment. Many of us have way more than we need and are holding on to clutter that no longer serves us.

Declutter your home. Declutter your mind. Declutter your life.

I believe that our environment is a direct reflection of the state of our mind, and vice versa. Clear out your space and keep it organized. Donate what you aren't using. Spend less time consuming, in person and online. Meditate and commit to practices that relax your mind each day. Open up more space on all levels!

This past year I've been challenging myself to commit to no new clothes (#nonewclothes) and it's been very liberating. I didn't realize until now how often I'd jump to purchase clothing I didn't need and would hardly ever end up wearing. I'll admit I haven't been perfect and have slipped a couple times, but the challenge has been great for my personal wellbeing and bank account. While I do love fashion and self expression in this way, I feel it's really important at this time on our planet to be more mindful of what we're purchasing and where it came from.

I've also committed to using as little plastic as possible and only supporting brands that are eco-friendly. This includes clothing, makeup, cleaning products, food packaging and beauty products. I always choose to support local artisans over larger corporations when possible.

So get to work, babe! Declutter your work space. Detail your car. Donate some clothes. Keep your altar and/or yoga space super clean and organized. An organized space is an organized mind. This opens up space to fully relax into your surroundings.

Let go on all levels and discover how freeing it is. What are you currently identifying with? Why are you holding onto things you don't use?

No matter what your current home looks like, this is your castle. How do the colours, items, and over all vibe in your castle make you feel? When you walk through the door do you feel alive and at peace? Do you feel empowered? Decorate it beautifully and in a way that makes you feel a close connection to Shakti.

FUTURE ROYAL MEMORIES

In Code III, I shared how I use the power of visualization to manifest my wildest dreams. Let's take our manifesting to the next level; the Empress level. It's my greatest hope for you that by this point in the book you realize your brilliance and believe in yourself more than ever before. You should now be able to not only see your future self clearly but feel her and her essence within you.

Meditate on your future Empress self, perhaps a year from this day. Get that vision in your mind's eye, then write a letter to your present day self from your future self. Date this letter one year (or your preferred date) from today. Channel your future powerful Empress self and share what steps you took to get where you are, get into every detail about your current life and don't miss a thing!

Breathe for a moment, welcome her in, and then free write for at least five minutes.

What does she want to tell you? What bold steps can you take today to get there? What does she want you to focus on? When you're done repeat what you've written out loud with conviction, as though it's your future high vibe boss babe self speaking it to you.

How can you begin to embody her essence right now?

Now, let's take it one step further and record a voice memo in your phone from your future self. Explain a day in your life. When you're done you can edit this voice file with some uplifting background music and let this be your daily affirmations for the next forty days. Some say you can change your life by committing to something for twenty-one days, I believe that in order for it to really make an impact, make it forty.

THE TANTRIC WHEEL OF LIFE

Let's work on designing your Empire. Evaluate and rate each area of your life on a scale of 1-10. Record your answers. Create at least two intentions for each area of your life. What steps can you take to raise the number in each area?

"To be creative means to be in love with life. You can be creative only if you love life enough that you want to enhance its beauty, you want to bring a little more music to it, a little more poetry to it, a little more dance to it."

— Osho

Be the Artist of your days.

Design the Empire beyond your wildest dreams.

YOUR ROYAL INITIATION

Just in case you've somehow missed it, here it is again; you can be whatever and whoever the fuck you want to be. If you are ready to step into your fierce feminine unstoppable Highest Empowered Empress Frequency (and I assume you are after reading this book and making it this far!) Then let's do it sister.

I would be deeply humbled, honoured, and ecstatic to initiate you into this new chapter of sacred leadership and full embodiment of your Divine Feminine Essence. Again, that doesn't mean you won't slip up. This is a commitment to love yourself through it all, to have immeasurable compassion to yourself and others, and to rule your Empire as your own, not based off of what others expect or think of you. This is you taking full, unapologetic ownership of your one precious, epic, life.

To begin the process, clean and prepare your home (castle) as though the most important person in the world is visiting. If you just found out the Queen of England had to visit your home tonight, what actions would you take? Clean, sage, bring out the good dishes, make it look impeccable! Don't be lazy here. Prepare for a Queen. Then set up a sacred ritual space, perhaps by your altar. Have flowers, sage, candles, crystals, gifts from the earth, objects to honour the four directions and elements, and whatever else feels right for you.

You may want to purchase a specific crown for this self initiation. I order all of mine from Etsy. You can also use an energetic crown or create a crown mudra (hand position) with your hands on top of your head and all fingers touching, creating a triangle shape, to feel this energy above your crown chakra. This crown is specifically for this initiation and will be used in the future to remember your Empresshood.

You might want anointing oil or Holy, cleansed water. Really, I believe all water is sacred and Holy but you can decide. Intuitively you'll know how to set up your space. Journal whatever is coming up for you, perhaps what you're ready to release and how this new chapter of your life is going to look.

Be clear on your intentions. How will this transition better your life, those around you, and the collective? Meditate and visualize yourself fully in your Empress frequency.

When you're ready, crown yourself. Anoint yourself. Initiate yourself. You can imagine me or other sisters sitting around you in sacred circle, witnessing your beautiful transition, holding this space energetically for you. Know that you are supported in this initiation and new chapter moving forward.

End the ritual with a dance to celebrate! Blast some music, shake off the old and stand proudly in this new, powerful, you! I'm so proud of you sister. I can't wait for you to discover all the magical treasures waiting in this new phase of your life. It's going to be so incredible, I know it!

SELF REFLECTION

1. How do the social media accounts you follow make you feel? What are your favourite feminine accounts? What do you have in common with these women? How can you show up more like they do?

2. When and in what areas do you find yourself comparing your life to others? When do you feel jealousy? Why do you think this is?

3. What can you commit to today to help manage those feelings?

4. What steps are you taking now to call in your soul sisters?

5. Write out the attributes you are looking for in your dream sisters. Are you fully embodying these qualities yourself?

6. Where have you been giving your power away by comparing, playing small, or replaying limiting beliefs around other women?

7. What are you releasing before your initiation?

8. Explain this new chapter of Empresshood with as much clarity as possible, what it means to you personally, and how you will embody this new energy moving forward.

9. What are your standards in all areas of your life? What are your non-negotiables?

10. What is a full body "fuck YES" for you in all areas?

11. Are you settling? Where? How can you release this, rise up and stand in your sovereign power?

12. What does your most empowered life look like? What steps do you need to take to allow this version of yourself to come forth?

13. If you continued to settle, how would your life look in 5 years? 10 years? How would it look if you held the standard?

YOUR HIGHEST INTENTION
MOVING FORWARD

**What have you learned along this journey and
what will you create from here?**

A FINAL NOTE FROM MY HEART TO YOURS

Sweet Sister,

I want to thank you again for showing up, taking this journey and choosing to prioritize yourself and your pleasure. As I've said so many times, what we do individually affects the collective.

By choosing to love ourselves and step into our power, we uplift the world and give other women permission to do the same.

I'd be honoured to support you further, if you feel called to connect please take a look at my website for current offerings and free gifts. krystalaranyani.com. You can also find our *Empowered Empress Mystery School* there which I run a couple times per year.

If you enjoyed this book and found it useful along your journey, I'd be so grateful if you could hop on Amazon and leave a review. I read them all and love seeing how these words landed in your heart! Your support really does make a difference and means the world to me.

Now get out there, rule your Empire, and live your best life ever babe!

Love always,

Krystal x

Printed in Great Britain
by Amazon

78415164R00111